Let's go to hell.

BOOM! STUDIOS

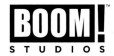

FAITH

LESS III

Story by
Brian Azzarello

Art by
Maria Llovet

Letters by
AndWorld Design

Published by
BOOM!
STUDIOS

Los Angeles, California

Designer
Michelle Ankley

Editor
Allyson Gronowitz

Executive Editor
Sierra Hahn

FAITHLESS Volume Three, November 2022. Published by BOOM! Studios, a division of Boom Entertainment, Inc. Faithless is ™ & © 2022 A Monkey Could Do This, LLC. Originally published in single magazine form as FAITHLESS III No. 1-6. ™ & © 2022 A Monkey Could Do This, LLC. All rights reserved. BOOM! Studios™ and the BOOM! Studios logo are trademarks of Boom Entertainment, Inc., registered in various countries and categories. All characters, events, and institutions depicted herein are fictional. Any similarity between any of the names, characters, persons, events, and/or institutions in this publication to actual names, characters, and persons, whether living or dead, events, and/or institutions is unintended and purely coincidental. BOOM! Studios does not read or accept unsolicited submissions of ideas, stories, or artwork

BOOM! Studios, 5670 Wilshire Boulevard, Suite 400, Los Angeles, CA 90036-5679. Printed in Hong Kong. First Printing.

ISBN: 978-1-68415-850-8, eISBN: 978-1-64668-597-4

The path to
paradise
begins in
hell.

Dante Alighieri

Chapter

One

I live for you.
But I'm not real. Not unless somebody believes in me.
That too vague? Let me explain...
I've been thinking about myself lately.
I've had some experiences--fabulous ones--all by my lonesome. (Which, by the way, I never am.)
Needless to say, I find myself to be a delightful companion.
But still.
Am I doing anything, if there are no witnesses?

I'm beginning to think I don't exist when I am alone.
On one hand it's a relief, because it's not easy being me.
But all that "me" time might as well have never happened, if there's no one there to see it.
Quite a conundrum...
See, I can't be what I am, if I'm not isolated.
And I'd rather you didn't know me, but invented me.

So, what are you
waiting for?

THE BLUE HOUSE Coffee
PING
Yo, Gin.
MARIA LLOVET 2021
Check it.
MoMA
LIVE
SCAM ARTIST?
GET THE FUCK OUT!
THE NUDE, BLOODY WOMAN FOUND IN THE MUSEUM OF MODERN ART BY GUARDS EARLY YESTERDAY HAS BEEN IDENTIFIED--
FAITH?
THE NOTORIOUS ARTIST **DISAPPEARED** JUST OVER NINE MONTHS AGO IN TURIN, ITALY...

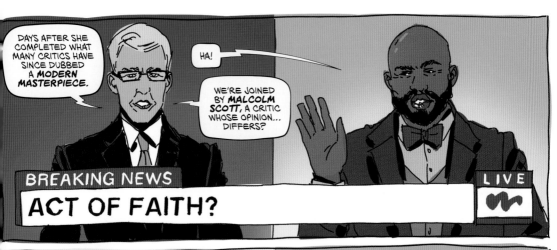

DAYS AFTER SHE COMPLETED WHAT MANY CRITICS HAVE SINCE DUBBED A *MODERN* MASTERPIECE.

HA!

WE'RE JOINED BY *MALCOLM SCOTT*, A CRITIC WHOSE OPINION... DIFFERS?

BREAKING NEWS

ACT OF FAITH?

LIVE

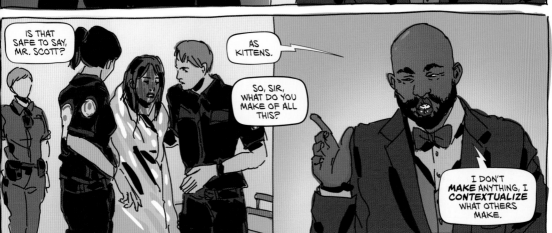

IS THAT SAFE TO SAY, MR. SCOTT?

AS KITTENS.

SO, SIR, WHAT DO YOU MAKE OF ALL THIS?

I DON'T *MAKE* ANYTHING, I *CONTEXTUALIZE* WHAT OTHERS MAKE.

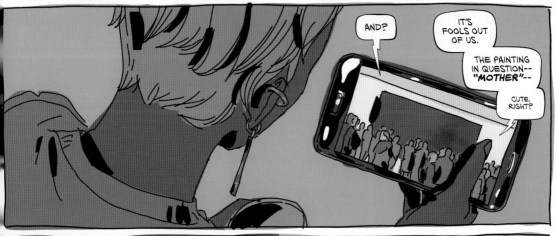

AND?

IT'S FOOLS OUT OF US.

THE PAINTING IN QUESTION-- *"MOTHER"*--

CUTE, RIGHT?

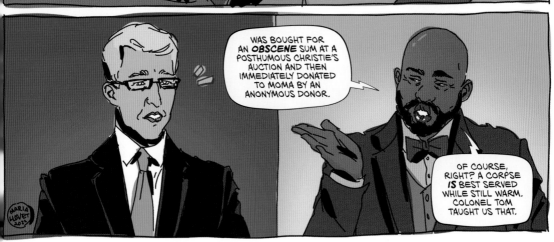

WAS BOUGHT FOR AN *OBSCENE* SUM AT A POSTHUMOUS CHRISTIE'S AUCTION AND THEN IMMEDIATELY DONATED TO MOMA BY AN ANONYMOUS DONOR.

OF COURSE, RIGHT? A CORPSE *IS* BEST SERVED WHILE STILL WARM. COLONEL TOM TAUGHT US THAT.

THE CIRCUMSTANCES WE'RE DISCUSSING--
YOU MEAN A NON-PROFIT INSTITUTION'S **CRAVEN** DESIRE TO MAKE A BUCK?
IT WAS HUNG--
NOT BY A NOOSE, WHICH IT DESERVED TO BE.
AND DEBATED.
BECAUSE MASTURBATION IS A TALENT IN THIS CULTURE.
UGH. FORGIVE ME FOR CALLING THIS **CESSPOOL** A CULTURE.
"MOTHER" IS AN EIGHTEEN-BY-NINE FOOT **TAMPON,** NOT A MASTERPIECE!
BUT--MAKE NO MISTAKE--THIS FAITH "ARTIST" WAS MEANT TO BE LOUIS THORN'S TRUE MASTERPIECE.
HE WANTED TO CREATE NOT ART, BUT AN ARTIST.
PITY SHE'S BEREFT OF ANY TALENT.
THOUGH IF--AND THIS IS A BIG IF--IT WAS THORN'S INTENTION TO CREATE SOMETHING WITH LESS TALENT THAN HE HAS?...
I STAND CORRECTED.
REPORTS STATE SHE WASN'T TAKEN TO THE HOSPITAL...

"...BUT TO **FIVE POINTS,** THORN'S MANHATTAN STUDIO. OPINION ON THAT, MALCOLM?"
"WELL, WHILE THE ART WORLD MIGHT CALL THIS PERFORMANCE...
"THE REAL WORLD CALLS IT A **PUBLICITY STUNT.**"
YOU HAVE NO IDEA HOW LUCKY YOU ARE TO BE IN HERE.
WHAT ARE YOU SAYIN'?
I'VE BEEN WAITING TWO WEEKS!
I KNOW.
FAITH MUST REALLY WANT TO SEE YOU.
I HEARD SHE CAME TO LIFE WHEN SHE HEARD YOUR NAME--GINNY, RIGHT? WHICH, BY THE WAY-- I LOVE LOVE **LOVE...**
MARIA LLOVET 2021

REMINDS ME OF AFTERNOONS IN REGGIO...
"GIN E TONIC, PER FAVORE."
LOVE
WHAT DO YOU MEAN, "CAME TO LIFE"?
LUS
LUST
YEAH. UM...YOU'RE ABOUT TO FIND OUT.
MARIA LLOVET 2021

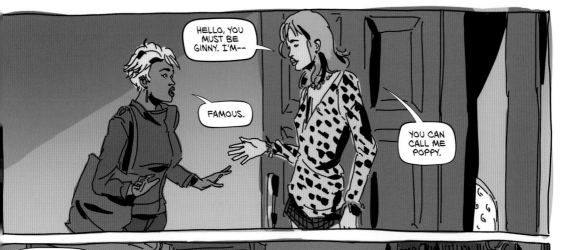

HELLO, YOU MUST BE GINNY. I'M--

FAMOUS.

YOU CAN CALL ME POPPY.

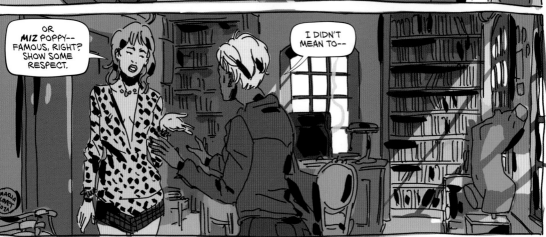

OR *MIZ* POPPY-- FAMOUS, RIGHT? SHOW SOME RESPECT.

I DIDN'T MEAN TO--

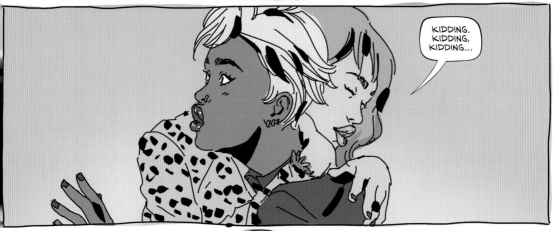

KIDDING. KIDDING, KIDDING...

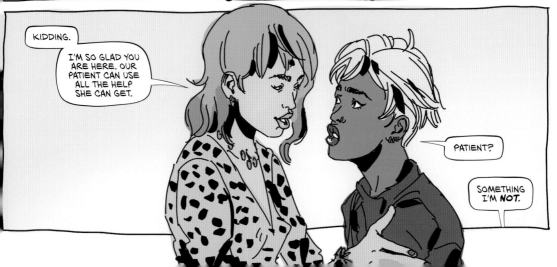

KIDDING.

I'M SO GLAD YOU ARE HERE. OUR PATIENT CAN USE ALL THE HELP SHE CAN GET.

PATIENT?

SOMETHING I'M *NOT*.

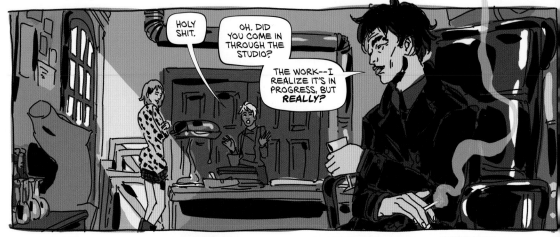

HOLY SHIT.

OH. DID YOU COME IN THROUGH THE STUDIO?

THE WORK--I REALIZE IT'S IN PROGRESS, BUT *REALLY?*

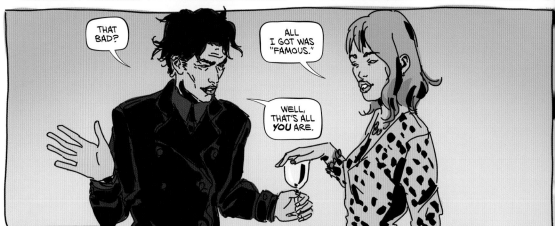

THAT BAD?

ALL I GOT WAS "FAMOUS."

WELL, THAT'S ALL *YOU* ARE.

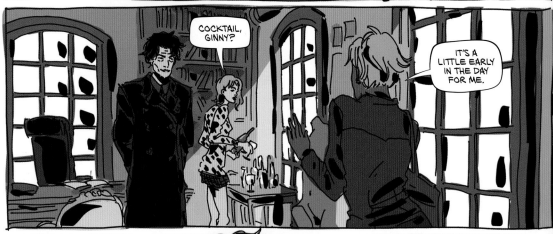

COCKTAIL, GINNY?

IT'S A LITTLE EARLY IN THE DAY FOR ME.

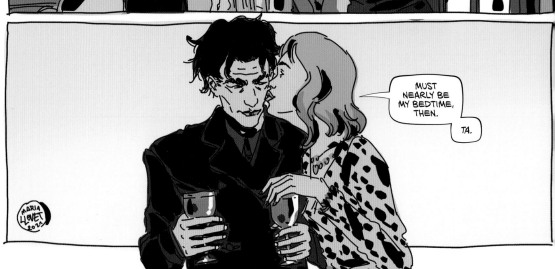

MUST NEARLY BE MY BEDTIME, THEN.

TA.

SO, GINNY, WELCOME TO THE FIVE POINTS. WHAT DO YOU THINK?
WELL, MISTER THORN--
NO, CALL ME...
...
I DO LIKE MISTER THORN.
IT'S BREATHTAKING.
JUST BREATH?
HMM.
FAITH?
YOU HAVE A VISITOR.
MARIA LLOVET 2021

FAITH?
GINNY?
I'M SO HAPPY TO SEE YOU.
...
YOU'RE NOT EVEN LOOKING AT ME.
THE CANVAS IS A MIRROR.
MARIA LLOVET 2021
NO SHIT? HOW COME I CAN'T SEE--
IT'S NOT YOUR CANVAS.
RIGHT...
C'MERE.

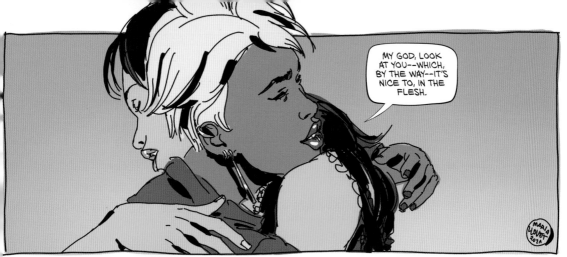

MY GOD, LOOK AT YOU—WHICH, BY THE WAY—IT'S NICE TO, IN THE FLESH.

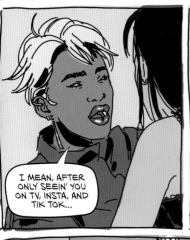

I MEAN, AFTER ONLY SEEIN' YOU ON TV, INSTA, AND TIK TOK...

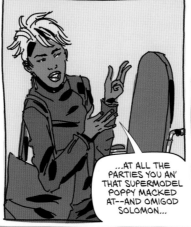

...AT ALL THE PARTIES YOU AN' THAT SUPERMODEL POPPY MACKED AT—AND OMIGOD SOLOMON...

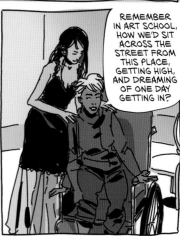

REMEMBER IN ART SCHOOL, HOW WE'D SIT ACROSS THE STREET FROM THIS PLACE, GETTING HIGH, AND DREAMING OF ONE DAY GETTING IN?

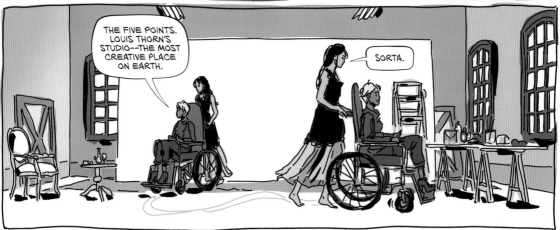

THE FIVE POINTS. LOUIS THORN'S STUDIO—THE MOST CREATIVE PLACE ON EARTH.

SORTA.

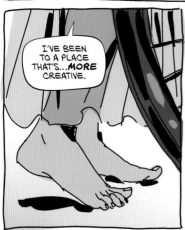

I'VE BEEN TO A PLACE THAT'S...*MORE* CREATIVE.

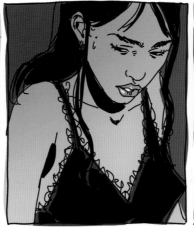

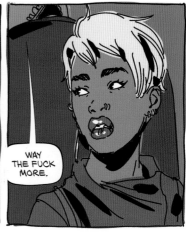

WAY THE FUCK MORE.

MARIA LLOVET 2021
GIRL, ARE YOU OKAY?
I THINK SO.
KINDA BORED.
OH. EXCUSE ME.
NO, I MEAN... YES.
GINNY, IT'S NOT YOU.
WHERE WERE YOU HIDING FOR ALMOST A YEAR?
I WASN'T HIDING.
I WAS...

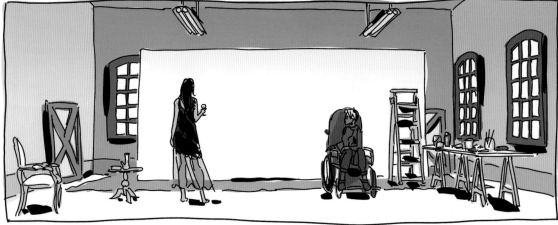

FAITH?
?
...WORDS DON'T COME EASILY.
I GUESS THAT'S WHY YOU'RE AN ARTIST.
YEAH. I GUESS THAT'S...
MARIA LLOVET 2021

THANK YOU, GINNY.
THANK YOU SO MUCH.
I KNEW YOU COULD HELP ME.
I NEED TO GET TO WORK.
THAT'S IT? NO "ARE THINGS BETTER WITH YOU AND RAY?"
OR "HOW'S JACOB? DOES HE LIKE SCHOOL?"
OR "NICE TO SEE YOU, GINNY, HOW WAS IT MAKING COFFEE WHILE I BECAME THE DARLING OF THE ART WORLD?"
FAITH--YOU DISAPPEARED FOR ALMOST A YEAR. I THOUGHT YOU WERE GONE FOR GOOD--DEAD--LIKE MAX AND AYA!
JACOB'S IN SCHOOL?
MARIA LLOVET 2021
BUT THE LAST TIME I SAW HIM HE WAS...
JUST A...
BABY?
JUST A BABY!
HE WAS ONLY A BABY!
"SO, FAITH IS FREAKING OUT AND MY PHONE RINGS--"
BZZZ
BZZZ
BZZZ

AND IT'S JACOB'S SCHOOL TELLING ME HE HAD AN ACCIDENT ON THE PLAYGROUND.
HE'S OKAY?
RAY, I TOLD YOU ALREADY, HE'S OKAY.
AIN'T YOU, BABY?
BACK TO WHAT I WAS SAYIN', FAITH IS OUT OF HER HEAD, BUT WITH JACOB BEING HURT, SO AM I, SO I GOT TO GO--
I GOTTA GO.
I'M AT THE ELEVATOR, AND FAITH IS PRACTICALLY WRAPPED AROUND MY ANKLES WHEN THE DOOR OPENS.
MOM! I REALLY GOTTA GO!

IT OPENS, AND THERE'S THORN LIKE HE'S BEEN STANDING THERE THE **WHOLE** TIME.
I'M NOT A LADY.
MARIA LLOVET 2021
I KNOW, BABY, BUT--
HE AIN'T GONNA BUDGE, GIN.
HELLO?
HELLO?
ALL CLEAR. LITTLE MAN, DO YOUR BUSINESS.

SO LOUIS FUCKING THORN, WHILE I'M FRANTIC, SAYS HE'S CURIOUS ABOUT WHAT IT'S LIKE TO BE A MOTHER, BECAUSE THAT'S SOMETHING HE COULD NEVER BE--WORRYING ALL THE TIME.
AND I'M LIKE--
JACOB. WHAT'S YOURS?
WHAT THE FUCK?
THAT'S FUNNY.
I'D BE, TOO.
NO, RAY...
MARIA LLOVET 2021
JACOB?

JACOB, IT'S MOM. WHO YOU TALKING TO, HONEY? IS EVERYTHING--
MARIA LLOVET 2021
HISSSSS
AAHHHH

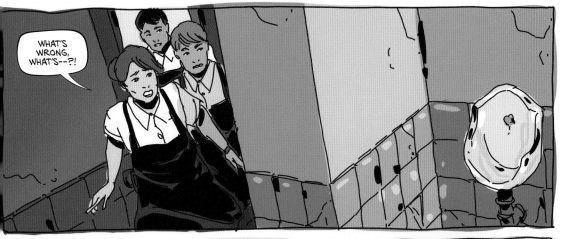

WHAT'S WRONG, WHAT'S--?!

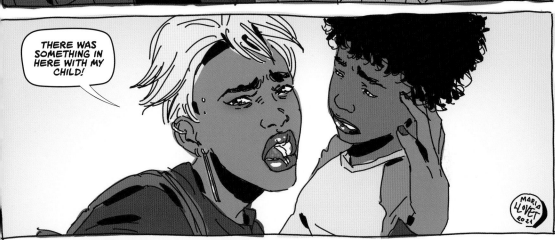

THERE WAS SOMETHING IN HERE WITH MY CHILD!

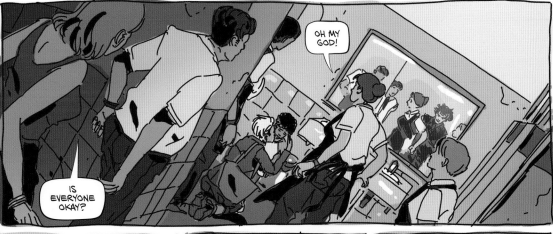

OH MY GOD!

IS EVERYONE OKAY?

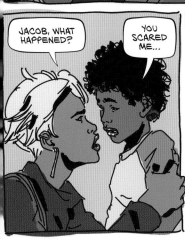

JACOB, WHAT HAPPENED?

YOU SCARED ME...

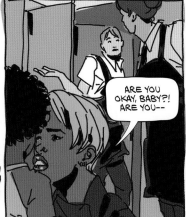

ARE YOU OKAY, BABY?! ARE YOU--

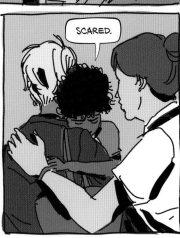

SCARED.

THAT'S ALL RIGHT--IT REALLY IS. LET'S GET THE BOTH OF YOU OUT OF HERE AND--
GET THEM SOME WATER...
AZZARELLO + LLOVET 2021

Art is what you can get away with.

Andy Warhol

Chapter

Two

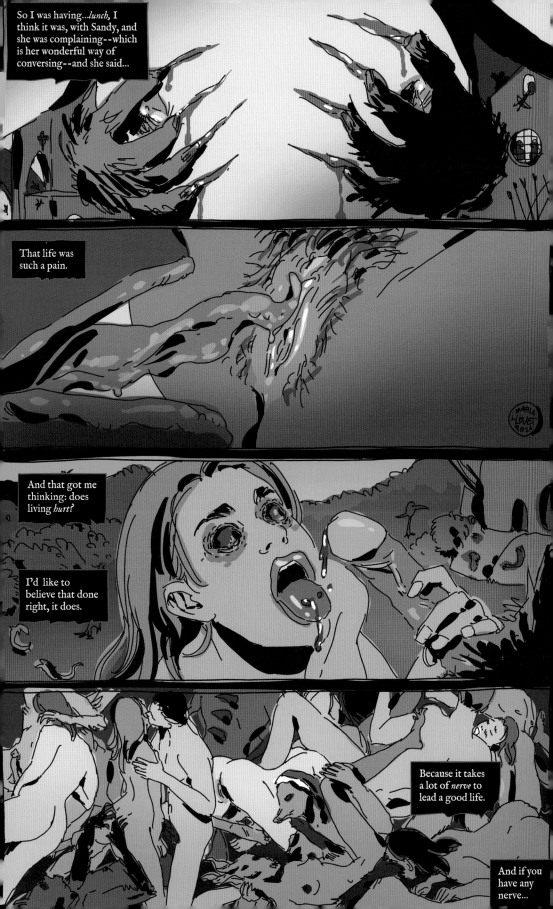

So I was having...*lunch,* I think it was, with Sandy, and she was complaining--which is her wonderful way of conversing--and she said...

That life was such a pain.

And that got me thinking: does living *hurt?*

I'd like to believe that done right, it does.

Because it takes a lot of *nerve* to lead a good life.

And if you have any nerve...

You're going to feel pain.
MARIA LLOVET 2021
So I guess the real question is, then: is life worth the pain you must endure to live it?
And assuming the answer is *yes*-- because there isn't anyone--
Anyone alive--
Who isn't afraid to die...
Then is the point of life to *suffer*, so that its end...
Can be *happy*?

If you ask *me*, I hope not.
Life should be all about *pleasures*.
But pleasures can be many things.
Some unknown...
Some never ending...
And some...
MARIA LLOVET 2021

Literally mean.

MARIA LLOVET 2021

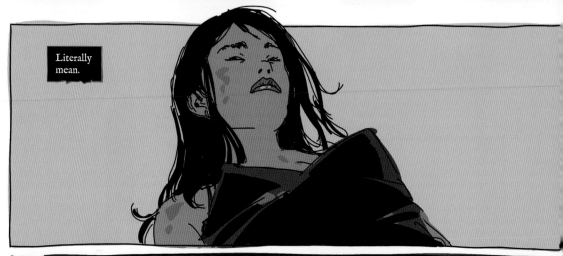

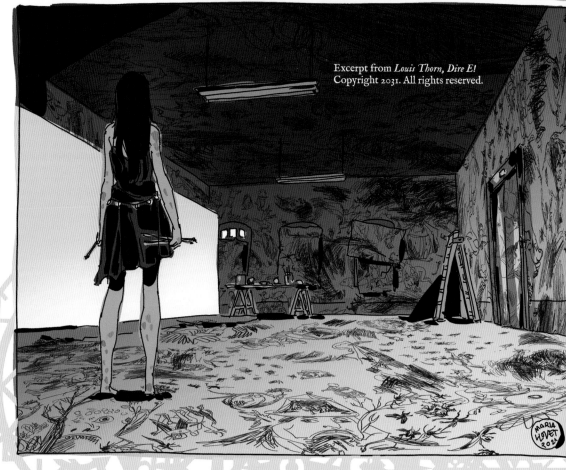

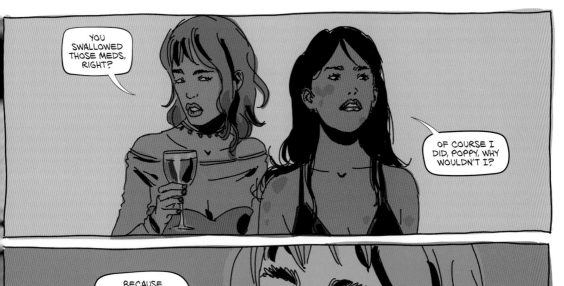

YOU SWALLOWED THOSE MEDS, RIGHT?

OF COURSE I DID, POPPY, WHY WOULDN'T I?

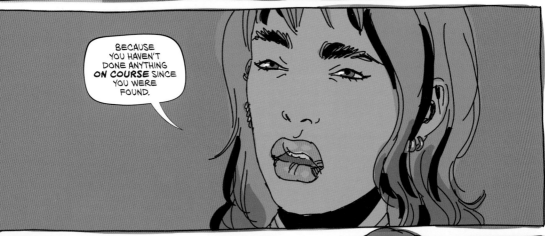

BECAUSE YOU HAVEN'T DONE ANYTHING **ON COURSE** SINCE YOU WERE FOUND.

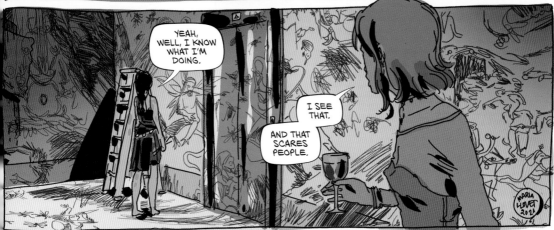

YEAH, WELL, I KNOW WHAT I'M DOING.

I SEE THAT.

AND THAT SCARES PEOPLE.

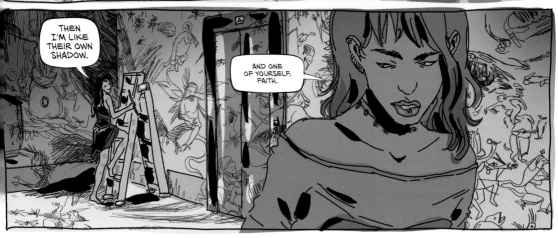

THEN I'M LIKE THEIR OWN SHADOW.

AND ONE OF YOURSELF, FAITH.

I DON'T LIKE HAVING TO BE RESPONSIBLE. IT DOESN'T SUIT ME.
THEN STOP IT, POPPY, AND JUST LET THE GIRL BE.
BE WHAT?
MARIA LLOVET 21
GLORIOUS.
SHE'S HUNTING FOR SOMETHING.
WHAT IF SHE FINDS IT?
SHE WON'T. BUT THAT'S WHAT LIFE *IS* FOR AN ARTIST.
AN ALL-CONSUMING SEARCH...
THEN DEATH.
THERE'S A CERTAIN PREDICTABILITY IN THE UNPREDICTABLE.
YOU GOT THAT RIGHT.

MARIA LLOVET 2021
LOUIS...
DADDY, I'M WORRIED. SHE'S MANIC.
NO...
SHE'S HITTING HER STRIDE.
LOOK AT HER...
SHE UNDERSTANDS...
SHE CAN LIVE FOREVER.
EVEN IF IT KILLS HER?

FAITH?
YES?
MARIA LLOVET 2021
WHAT DO YOU SAY WE GO AWAY FOR A WHILE? DO YOU SOME GOOD TO GET OUT OF HERE.
SOLOMON'S TOURING AGAIN...
HE IS? SOUNDS LIKE FUN.
YOU SHOULD GO.
POPPY...
SHE DOESN'T UNDERSTAND WHAT YOU'RE DOING.
AND YOU DO?
DRRR
THE STRUGGLE...?
I DO.
THEN BY THE POWER INFESTED IN ME, I NOW PRONOUNCE US MAN AND--
SHH HH

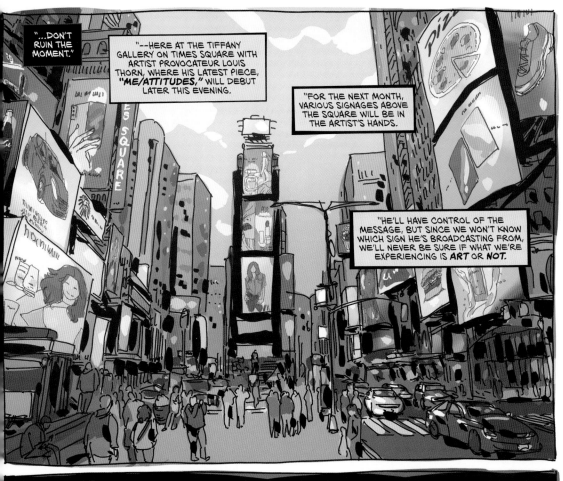

"...DON'T RUIN THE MOMENT."

"--HERE AT THE TIFFANY GALLERY ON TIMES SQUARE WITH ARTIST PROVOCATEUR LOUIS THORN, WHERE HIS LATEST PIECE, **"ME/ATTITUDES,"** WILL DEBUT LATER THIS EVENING.

"FOR THE NEXT MONTH, VARIOUS SIGNAGES ABOVE THE SQUARE WILL BE IN THE ARTIST'S HANDS.

"HE'LL HAVE CONTROL OF THE MESSAGE, BUT SINCE WE WON'T KNOW WHICH SIGN HE'S BROADCASTING FROM, WE'LL NEVER BE SURE IF WHAT WE'RE EXPERIENCING IS **ART** OR **NOT.**

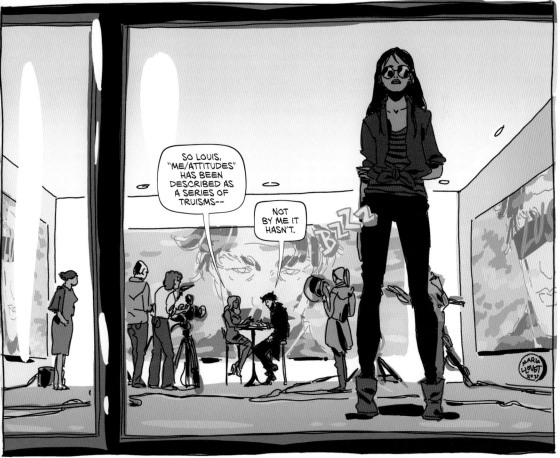

SO LOUIS, "ME/ATTITUDES" HAS BEEN DESCRIBED AS A SERIES OF TRUISMS--

NOT BY ME IT HASN'T.

BZZZ

I MEAN, DON'T YOU **LOATHE** THE TRUTH? IT'S SO DULL.
Hey
Hey
Where are you?
SO YOU PREFER A *FAÇADE*?
DO I? HMM...
Times Square
WTF?
Louis asked me to come to his interview
I FIND THEM TO BE MORE HONEST, I GUESS.
BUT THEN, DON'T WE ALL?
I'm not far.
Cum meet me
I cnt
WHAT PEOPLE **PRESENT** THEMSELVES TO BE IS SO MUCH MORE INTERESTING THAN WHAT THEY TRULY ARE.
I'll make it worth your while.
Where are you?

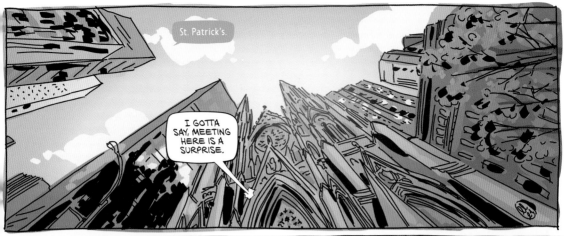

St. Patrick's.

I GOTTA SAY, MEETING HERE IS A SURPRISE.

I WANTED TO BE SOMEPLACE DADDY WOULDN'T THINK OF.

GOOD CHOICE, THEN.

LISTEN, FAITH...

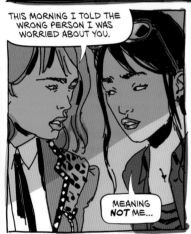

THIS MORNING I TOLD THE WRONG PERSON I WAS WORRIED ABOUT YOU.

MEANING *NOT* ME...

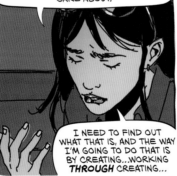

IT'S HARD TO DESCRIBE HOW I FEEL, POPPY. IT'S LIKE I LOST A YEAR, AND I DON'T CARE, BUT THERE'S SOMETHING MISSING NOW THAT I *DO* CARE ABOUT.

I NEED TO FIND OUT WHAT THAT IS, AND THE WAY I'M GOING TO DO THAT IS BY CREATING...WORKING *THROUGH* CREATING...

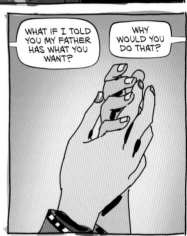

WHAT IF I TOLD YOU MY FATHER HAS WHAT YOU WANT?

WHY WOULD YOU DO THAT?

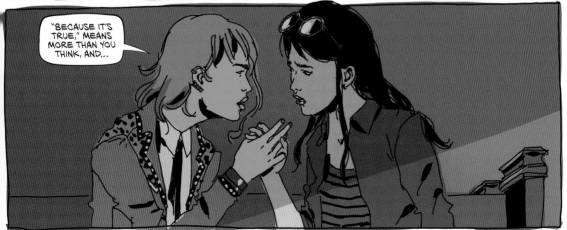

"BECAUSE IT'S TRUE," MEANS MORE THAN YOU THINK, AND...

BECAUSE I MISS YOU.
OH MY GOD, WHAT ARE YOU DOING?
...
PREYING.
HAHA--
SHHH...
BE IN THE MOMENT.
THIS IS SO WRONG...
MARIA LLOVET 2021
RIGHT?
TELL ME HOW IT FEELS.
INRI
IT FEELS...

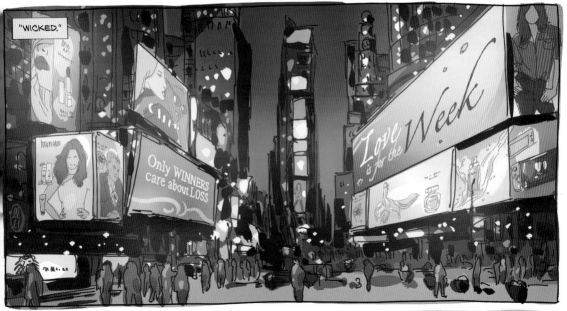

"WICKED."

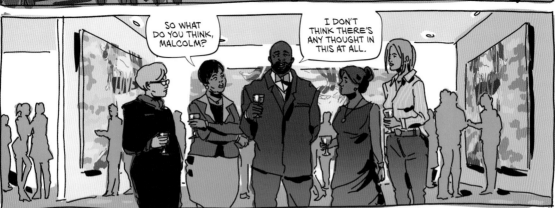

SO WHAT DO YOU THINK, MALCOLM?

I DON'T THINK THERE'S ANY THOUGHT IN THIS AT ALL.

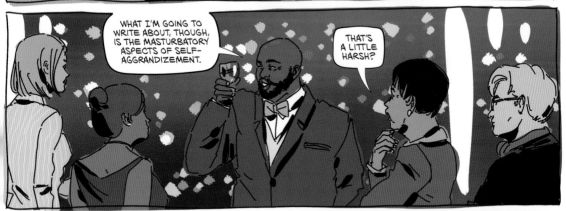

WHAT I'M GOING TO WRITE ABOUT, THOUGH, IS THE MASTURBATORY ASPECTS OF SELF-AGGRANDIZEMENT.

THAT'S A LITTLE HARSH?

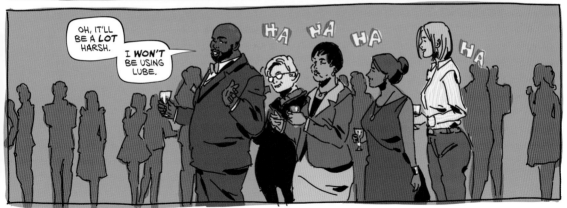

OH, IT'LL BE A *LOT* HARSH. I *WON'T* BE USING LUBE.

HA HA HA HA

"TIMES SQUARE DISAPPOINTS ME."
LUST IS THE GOAL
PIZZA
IT USED TO BE SO EXCITING AND SEEDY. NOW THIS **SPECTACLE...**
I'VE ADAPTED, BUT LET ME TELL YOU, I'D RATHER HAVE A COUPLE HUSTLERS WALKING THE STREETS MUMBLING TO PASSERSBY ABOUT WHAT I'M SELLING.
BUT WOULDN'T YOU SAY THAT THIS IS **SOCIAL MEDIA** TAKEN TO ITS LOGICAL CONCLUSION?
ABSOLUTELY NOT.
"IT'S BIGGER...
Don't LOOK at me
"BUT SMALLER."
SCOPE, MEET SCALE.
I MEAN...

WHAT'S THE POINT?
JUST A SPLASH.
HAVE YOU SEEN WHAT FAITH'S BEEN UP TO?
WELL, YOU CAN'T UNSEE GENIUS, AND IT'S FUCKING BRILLIANT.
SO YEAH, I'VE SEEN IT.
ON THE D.L.? NOBODY ELSE WILL.
LOUIS IS JEALOUS N'SHIT. THAT WORK AIN'T LEAVING FIVE POINTS.
FER REAL?
WHAT PART OF GENIUS DON'T YOU UNDERSTAND?
HA. SO YOU HITTIN' THE AFTER-PARTY?
GIRL...
MARIA LLOVET 2021

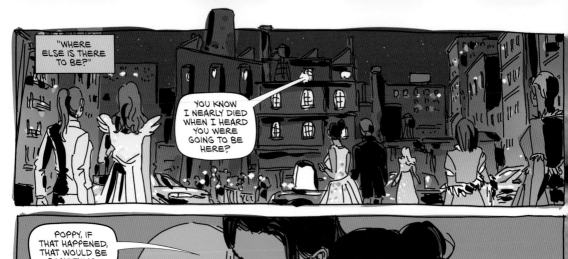

"WHERE ELSE IS THERE TO BE?"

YOU KNOW I NEARLY DIED WHEN I HEARD YOU WERE GOING TO BE HERE?

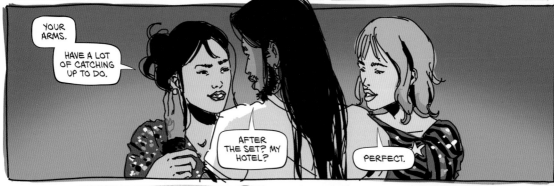

POPPY, IF THAT HAPPENED, THAT WOULD BE SOMETHING.

SO GOOD TO SEE YOU, SOLOMON...

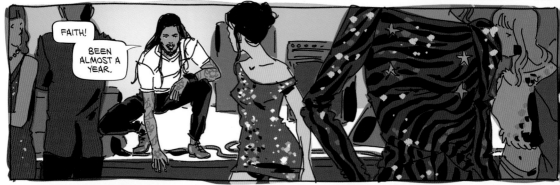

YOUR ARMS.

HAVE A LOT OF CATCHING UP TO DO.

AFTER THE SET? MY HOTEL?

PERFECT.

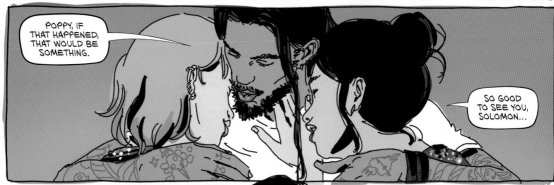

FAITH!

BEEN ALMOST A YEAR.

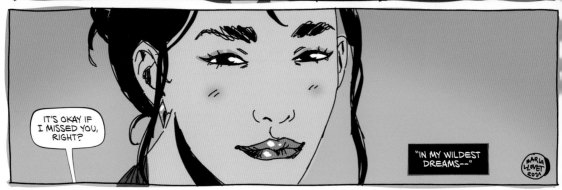

IT'S OKAY IF I MISSED YOU, RIGHT?

"IN MY WILDEST DREAMS--"

AND MY NIGHTMARES.
--I NEVER BELIEVED I'D SEE YOU HERE AGAIN, MALCOLM. NOT AFTER THE LAST TIME, IN JUST YOUR UNDERWEAR.
WELL THEN, LOUIS, I GUESS DREAMS DO COME TRUE.
IT'S BEEN WHAT? THIRTY-SOME YEARS SINCE I'VE BEEN HERE LAST?
OR THAT WE'VE SPOKEN.
WELL, WE'RE ALWAYS ON EACH OTHER'S TONGUES.
SPEAK FOR YOURSELF.
LIAR.
MARIA LLOVET 2021
FLATTERY WILL GET YOU NOWHERE.
DUM DUM DUM DUM

DUM DUM
THOSE SIX NOTES GET ME SO WET.
DUM
POPPY, WITH LOUIS...ISN'T THAT...
WE'RE **THE WISDOM!**
WELCOME BACK.
DOS, TRES, CUATRO--
LET'S GO.
BUT HE'S JUST GETTING STARTED.
BUT I...
CAN'T WAIT.

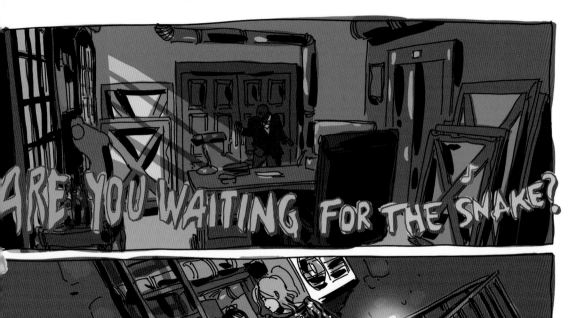

ARE YOU WAITING FOR THE SNAKE?

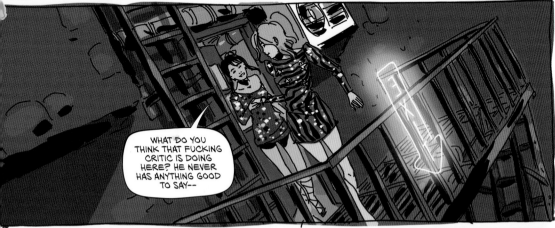

WHAT DO YOU THINK THAT FUCKING CRITIC IS DOING HERE? HE NEVER HAS ANYTHING GOOD TO SAY--

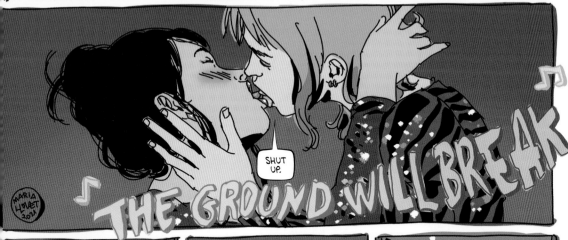

SHUT UP.

THE GROUND WILL BREAK

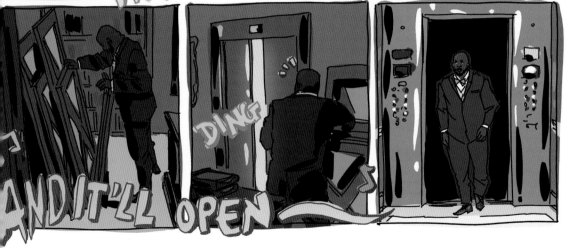

DING!

AND IT'LL OPEN

ARE YOU ACHING ON THE MAKE?
DING
EV'RY BREATH YOU TAKE
BELONGS TO SOMEONE
MY GOD...
MARIA LLOVET 2021
EXTRAORDINARY.
GENIUS...
"JUST GENIUS."
DO WHAT YOU WANT
I SAID DO
...?
WHAT YOU

DO WHAT YOU WANT ♪ I SAID DO ♪
WHAT YOU ♪
NO ONE'S WATCHING ♪
POPPY...?
MARIA LLOVET 2021

THAT LAST NIGHT IN TURIN...I REMEMBER NOW...
I WAS **PREGNANT.** WHEN I WAS GONE...
I HAD A BABY.
I KNOW.
EXIT
AZZARELLO + LOVET 2021

We are each our own **devil,** and we make this world our **hell.**

Oscar Wilde

Chapter
Three

I CAN'T--
I'M SO HAPPY-- SERIOUSLY--I MEAN, I'VE BEEN DYING TO TELL YOU.
WHY DIDN'T YOU TELL ME?
WHERE'S THE FUN IN THAT?
MARIA LLOVET 2021
I HAD A BABY...
NO, YOU HAVE A BABY.
WHERE IS...
HE? SHE? WHAT FLAVOR...?
NEVER CHANGED ITS DIAPER, SO I DON'T KNOW.

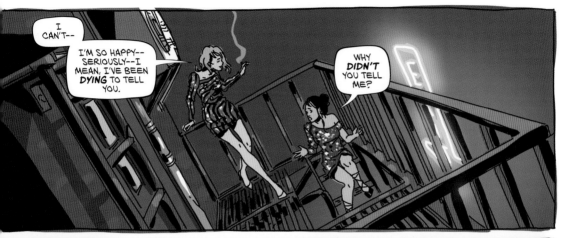

"ITS"? JESUS CHRIST, DOES "ITS" HAVE A NAME?
AIN'T J.C., I CAN TELL YOU THAT.
LOOK, THE I.D. STUFF, I DON'T KNOW. HONESTLY, I'M NOT INTERESTED IN ANY OF IT...
BUT I AM *IN* ALL OF YOU.
NOW YOU KNOW--SO LET'S MOVE ON.
WE NEED TO LEAVE. I NEED TO GET YOU OUT OF HERE.
I'M NOT GOING ANYWHERE!

FAITH...

CLON CLON

IT'S MAGIC. ALL A TRICK.

DON'T FALL FOR IT.

DON'T FALL? DON'T FALL? WHO EXACTLY IS TELLING ME NOT TO--

ZAH

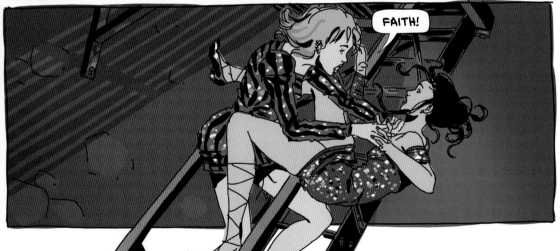

FAITH!

LOUIS!
WHERE IS MY BABY?
YOUR BABY?
LAST TIME I CHECKED, IT TOOK TWO TO TANGLE.
AND WHAT MAKES YOU THINK I WOULD HAVE "YOUR" BABY?
BECAUSE YOU HAVE **EVERYTHING!**
OH.
YES, I DO.

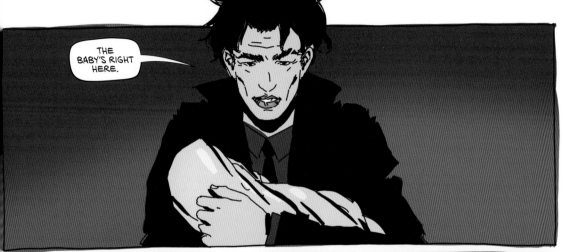

THE BABY'S RIGHT HERE.

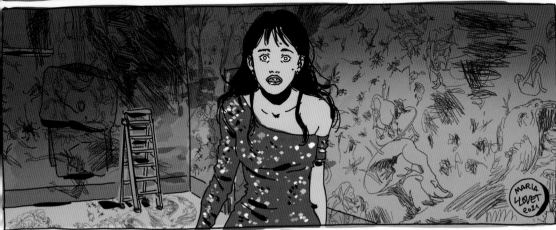

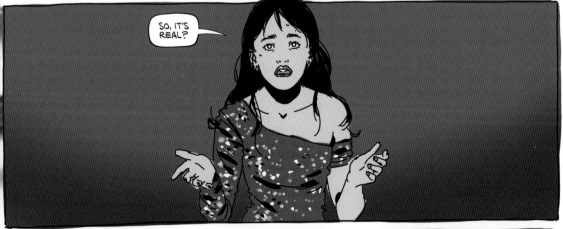

SO, IT'S REAL?

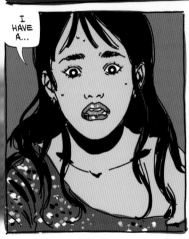

I HAVE A...

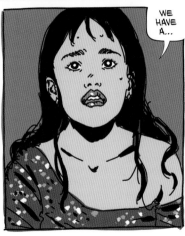

WE HAVE A...

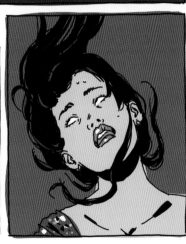

MARIA LLOVET 2021
WE?

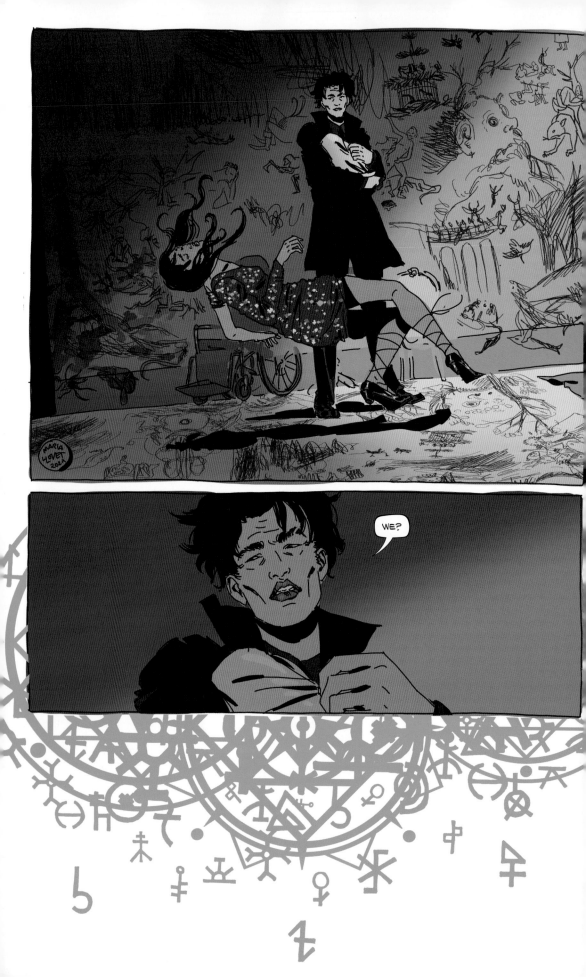

My mother and I share a special bond. My own insatiable curiosity, I think, comes from her.
That woman...
Every time a door is locked, all I hear from her is, "What are you doing in there?"
I'm just like her, too. It's not biological, but *pathological*--though, seriously, what's the difference?
Over the years, more than one therapist has said the difference is *big*, and admittedly, size *does* matter...
But your parents are either in your genes or your jeans, and in both places they aren't welcome.

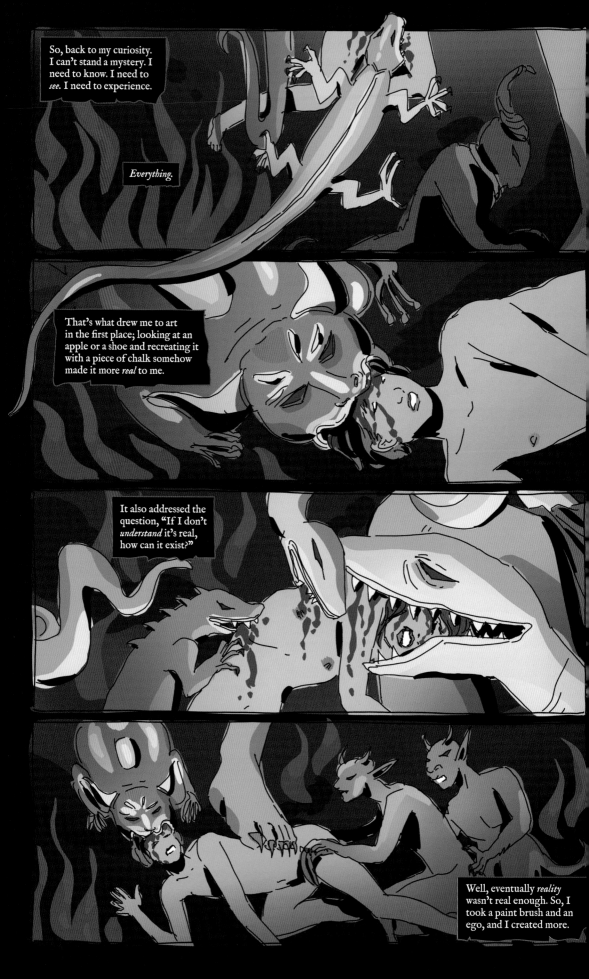

So, back to my curiosity. I can't stand a mystery. I need to know. I need to *see*. I need to experience.

Everything.

That's what drew me to art in the first place; looking at an apple or a shoe and recreating it with a piece of chalk somehow made it more *real* to me.

It also addressed the question, "If I don't *understand* it's real, how can it exist?"

Well, eventually *reality* wasn't real enough. So, I took a paint brush and an ego, and I created more.

I *made* reality.

By the way, my mother died in childbirth.
Isn't that romantic?
Excerpt from *Louis Thorn, Dire E!*
Copyright 2031. All rights reserved.
MARIA LLOVET 2021

MARIA LLOVET 2021

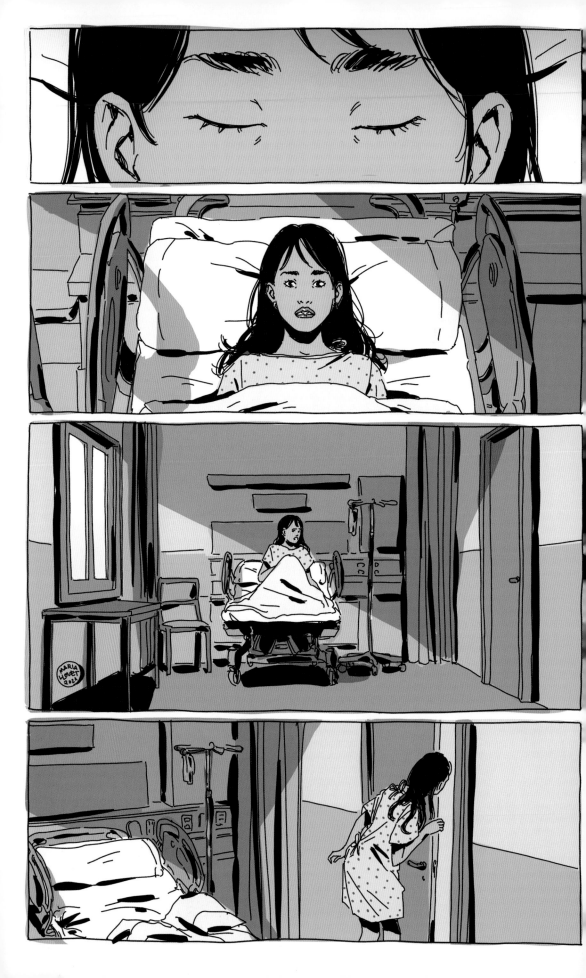

SO THIS BOY WON'T TAKE "NO," FOR AN ANSWER--
AN' I'M ALL, "BOY?"--
...AYA?
F-FAITH?!
OH MY GOD, FAITH!
MARIA LLOVET 2021
YOU'RE AWAKE!
YOU'RE ALIVE?
"ALL I GOTTA SAY, THIS IS SOME SERIOUSLY FREAKY WIZARD OF OZ SHIT."

MAX?!
I MEANT THAT IN A GOOD WAY!
THAT'S HOW I TOOK IT, TOO, GINNY.
I'M SORRY. YOU'RE NOT FRAGILE--I KNOW, BUT I'M A MOTHER...
DAMN RIGHT YOU ARE.
MARIA LLOVET 2021
I'M JUS' ROASTIN'.
CHRIST.
WAS HE IN YOUR DREAM?
JESUS...
I KNEW IT!
HE SEEMS LIKE HE'S THE KINDA DUDE I'D AVOID.

WHY'S THAT?
I DUNNO... I DON'T TRUST NICE PEOPLE.
BUT YOU BELIEVE IN GOD?
MAYBE. I'LL RESERVE JUDGMENT UNTIL FAITH ANSWERS MAX'S QUESTION.
WELL?
I CAN'T TELL YOU--
FUCK-- C'MON!
--HOW GREAT IT IS TO BE WITH ALL OF YOU AGAIN!
"I'M SO JEALOUS OF GINNY."

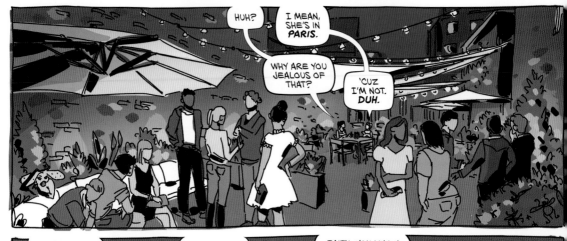

HUH?

I MEAN, SHE'S IN *PARIS*.

WHY ARE YOU JEALOUS OF THAT?

'CUZ I'M NOT. *DUH.*

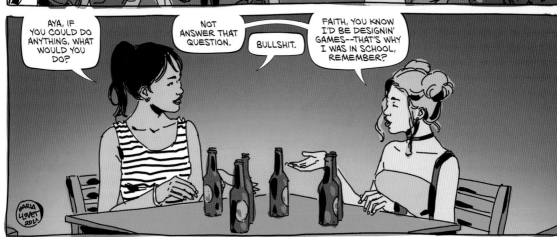

AYA, IF YOU COULD DO ANYTHING, WHAT WOULD YOU DO?

NOT ANSWER THAT QUESTION.

BULLSHIT.

FAITH, YOU KNOW I'D BE DESIGNIN' GAMES--THAT'S WHY I WAS IN SCHOOL, REMEMBER?

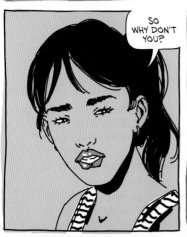

SO WHY DON'T YOU?

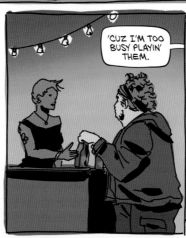

'CUZ I'M TOO BUSY PLAYIN' THEM.

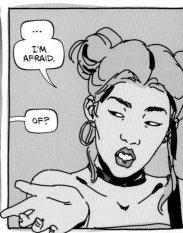

...

I'M AFRAID.

OF?

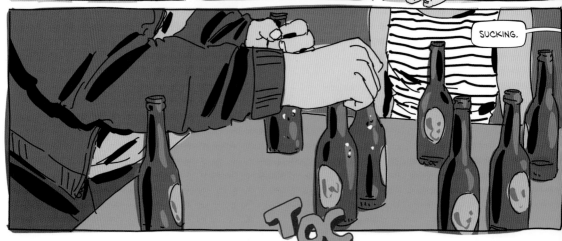

SUCKING.

TOC

YOU BITCHES ALL ARE.
EXCUSE ME?
OH, NO--I DIDN'T MEAN THAT THE WAY YOU THINK I DID.
LOOK--I'M A BITCH TOO, AND WE ARE ALL AFRAID OF SUCKING.
ART SCHOOL MIGHTA BEEN WORTH ALL THE STUPID LOANS I HAVE TO PAY OFF IF THERE WAS A CLASS ON "HOW NOT TO SUCK."
KLIN!
YOU MEAN ON HOW NOT TO BE AFRAID.
OH, DO I, BITCH?
CAN YOU STOP SAYING THAT?
SURE...
MA'AM.
WOW.
SEE? BITCH AIN'T SO BAD, IS IT, BITCH?
MARIA LLOVET 2021

WHAT KIND OF A DORK SENDS POSTCARDS ANYMORE?
OUR DORK.
WHAT ARE YOU DRAWING?
THE TWO OF YOU.
LEMME SEE.
WHATEVER HAPPENED TO ALL THOSE WITCHY-POO, OCCULTY SYMBOLS YOU USED TO DO?
MEH, I GUESS I GOT BORED. REAL LIFE IS MAGIC ENOUGH, RIGHT?
SINCE WHEN?
HOW 'BOUT SINCE I WOKE UP FROM A COMA?
YEAH, OKAY, SURE. BUT THAT WAS... WHAT...
MARIA LLOVET 2021

NINE MONTHS AGO?
FUCK, MAN, TIME'S WEIRD.
LIKE IT FLIES AND STANDS STILL ALL AT ONCE.
I, AH...
I'M GONNA GET GOING.
SEE YOU LATER.
...
I LOVE YOU TWO.
MARIA LLOVET
ALL I SAID WAS "SEE YOU LATER"...
SOMETHIN' GOIN' ON I SHOULD KNOW ABOUT?

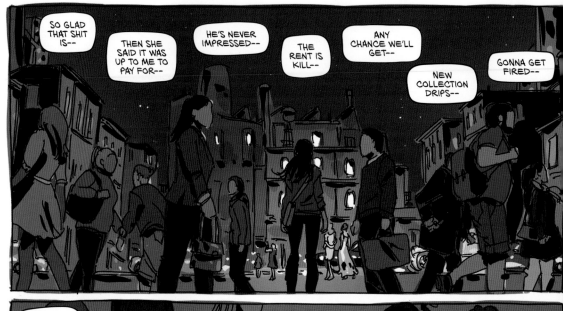

SO GLAD THAT SHIT IS--

THEN SHE SAID IT WAS UP TO ME TO PAY FOR--

HE'S NEVER IMPRESSED--

THE RENT IS KILL--

ANY CHANCE WE'LL GET--

NEW COLLECTION DRIPS--

GONNA GET FIRED--

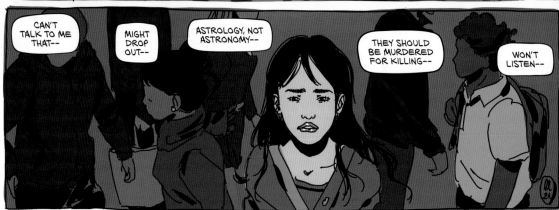

CAN'T TALK TO ME THAT--

MIGHT DROP OUT--

ASTROLOGY, NOT ASTRONOMY--

THEY SHOULD BE MURDERED FOR KILLING--

WON'T LISTEN--

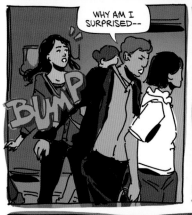

WHY AM I SURPRISED--

BUMP

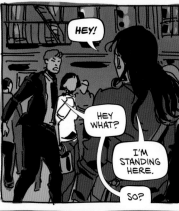

HEY!

HEY WHAT?

I'M STANDING HERE.

SO?

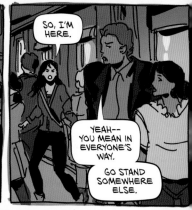

SO, I'M HERE.

YEAH-- YOU MEAN IN EVERYONE'S WAY.

GO STAND SOMEWHERE ELSE.

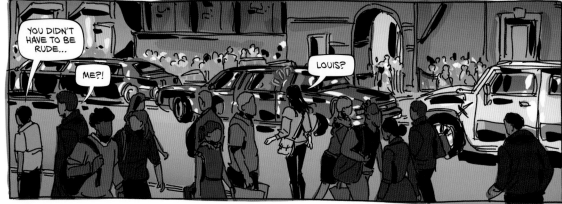

YOU DIDN'T HAVE TO BE RUDE...

ME?!

LOUIS?

MISS, PLEASE STAND--
LOUIS, CAN I TALK TO YOU?
DO YOU RECOGNIZE HER FROM ANYWHERE?
NO.
TV, TIK TOK, PORNO?
NO, SIR.
THEN SHE HAS NOTHING TO SAY, DOES SHE?
I'M THE GIRL WHO FELL OFF YOUR FIRE ESCAPE LAST SPRING.
THAT'S NICE, BUT MY LAWYER'S OFFICE ISN'T HERE.
IS MY BABY?

ARE YOU SURE YOU WANT TO DO THIS?
YES.
REMARKABLE. I GAVE YOU A WAY OUT...
OF?
REALITY.
WHY WOULD I WANT OUT OF REALITY?
BECAUSE YOU'RE HUMAN. ALL OF YOU LIVE TO ESCAPE IT.
SO YOU CREATED ONE FOR ME...?
MARIA LLOVET 2021

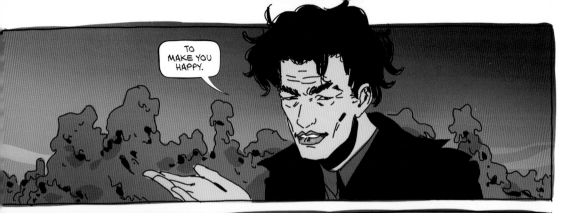

TO MAKE YOU HAPPY.

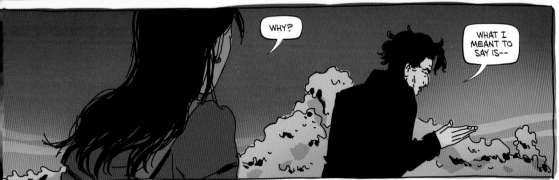

WHY?

WHAT I MEANT TO SAY IS--

EXACTLY WHAT YOU DID SAY.

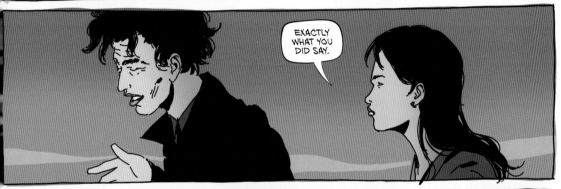

THAT, FAITH, NEVER HAPPENS.

YOUR BABY...

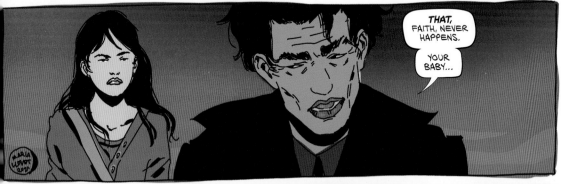

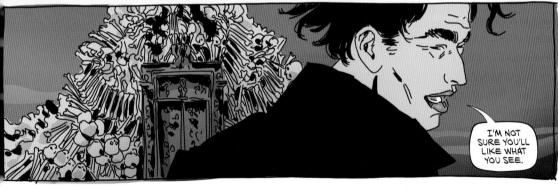

I'M NOT SURE YOU'LL LIKE WHAT YOU SEE.

REALLY? YOU HAVE THE SAME EYES?
WE DO.
AND CLOVEN FEET?
HEH.
PLEASE, DO COME INSIDE...
YOU BRIGHT, NASTY GIRL.
AZZARELLO + LLOVET 2021

I find only freedom in the realms of eccentricity.

David Bowie

Chapter
Four

"SO THIS IS HELL?"
"THIS? NO. THIS IS A DISTRACTION."
"A WHAT?"
"IT'S KITSCHY, RIGHT?"
"KITSCHY"? YOU HAVE A VERY SINISTER INTERPRETATION OF KITSCH...
MOI?
DON'T INSULT ME...
I DIDN'T CREATE HELL, JUST LIKE I DIDN'T BOMB HIROSHIMA.
"NO, THIS PASTICHE WAS SCHEMED UP BY SEDENTARY MONKS AND SYPHILITIC APES--
"FRIGHTENED MINDS DESPERATE TO KEEP THE WEAK ONES IN LINE."
MARIA LLOVET

"SO HELL ISN'T REAL?"
"OF COURSE IT IS. I MEAN, I DOUBT WE'D BE HAVING THIS CONVERSATION IF--"
WHAT'S **REAL** HELL?
SOMETHING YOU CAN'T UNDERSTAND.
MARIA LLOVET 2022
TRY ME.
I HAVE.
YES, YOU HAVE...
REAL HELL IS HAVING EXPERIENCED HEAVEN.
WHAT'S HEAVEN LIKE?

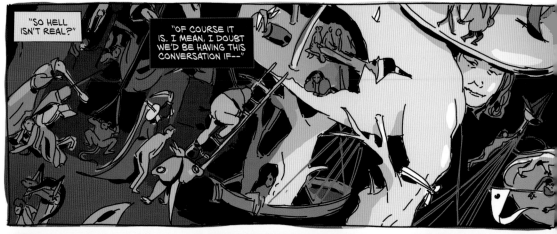

HAVE YOU EVER HAD YOUR HEART BROKEN?
EVERY BREAK-UP THAT **WASN'T** MY IDEA.
MARIA LLOVET 2022
OH.
YOU POOR DEAR.
RIGHT? **SO** MANY HURT FEELINGS...
BUT LIKE, REALLY HEARTBROKEN? I GUESS NOT.
FAITH, THERE'S NO **GUESSING** WHEN YOU HAVE.
OR **ESCAPING** IT.
"A BROKEN HEART IS LIKE A PHANTOM LIMB.
"WHAT'S GONE IS ALL YOU CAN FEEL...
BZZ
ZZZZZZ
"IT'S MORE OF AN AMPUTATION."
"THAT'S WHAT HEAVEN IS LIKE?"
BZZ
ZZZZ
"TO ME...?"

"YES, IT IS."
SOLOMON, I NEED TO TALK TO YOU.
MARIA LLOVET 2022

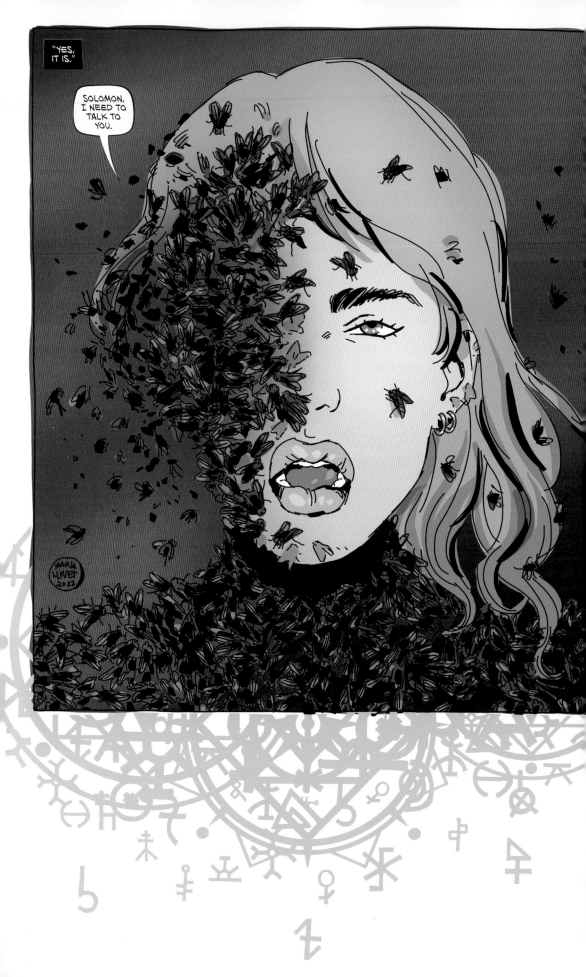

ABOUT?
I DON'T LIKE THE WAY THIS IS GOING.
JEALOUS?
AFRAID.
OH.
THAT'S DIFF--
DESPITE WHAT IT IS, I WOULD LIKE YOU TO DO SOMETHING ABOUT IT.
I'M NOT WELCOME THERE.
YOU ARE IF YOU'RE WITH ME.
BABY, MY LIGHT--
TRUST ME.
POPPY...

THAT'S ALWAYS BEEN A MISTAKE.
"YOU SEE, FAITH, IN HEAVEN BEING CREATIVE IS TRANSGRESSIVE. WHILE HERE, IT'S--"
CRSSSSS
IT'S WHAT, LOUIS?
?
WOULD YOU LIKE SOME WINE?

THIS IS AMAZING. WHAT IS IT?
JUST WATER. FROM CANA.
OR IT WAS, UNTIL A WEDDING, AND HE...
WORKED HIS MAGIC.
HMM.
I WONDER IF YOU CAN DO THAT.
ANYWAY, CREDIT WHERE CREDIT IS DUE. IT IS QUITE NICE. NOT THE BEST, BUT...
WE'LL SAVE THAT BOTTLE FOR SUPPER.
WE EAT IN HELL?
WE PREY.
SAME DIFFERENCE.

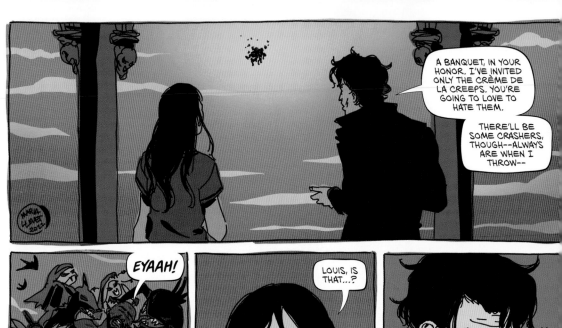

A BANQUET, IN YOUR HONOR. I'VE INVITED ONLY THE CRÈME DE LA CREEPS. YOU'RE GOING TO LOVE TO HATE THEM.

THERE'LL BE SOME CRASHERS, THOUGH--ALWAYS ARE WHEN I THROW--

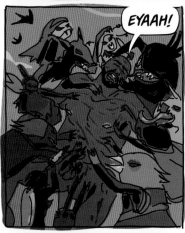

EYAAH!

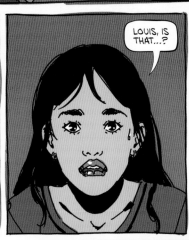

LOUIS, IS THAT...?

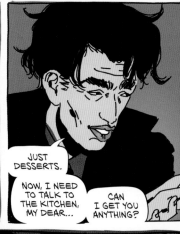

JUST DESSERTS.

NOW, I NEED TO TALK TO THE KITCHEN, MY DEAR...

CAN I GET YOU ANYTHING?

THE BABY, LOUIS.

OH, RIGHT.

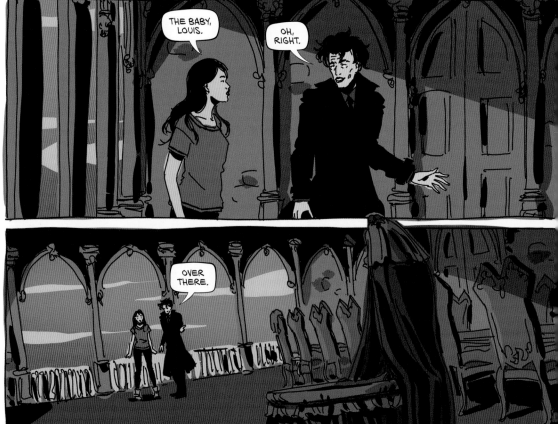

OVER THERE.

I'LL LEAVE YOU TWO TO GET ACQUAINTED.
HMM.
YOU'RE NOT WHAT I WAS EXPECT--
FAITH?
HUH!

SOLOMON...
MARIA LLOVET 22
YOU SHOULDN'T BE HERE.
NEITHER SHOULD YOU.
LET'S GO.
NO...
DOESN'T EVEN LOOK LIKE LOUIS.
HE THINKS THOSE ARE HIS EYES.
WE BETTER HOPE NOT.

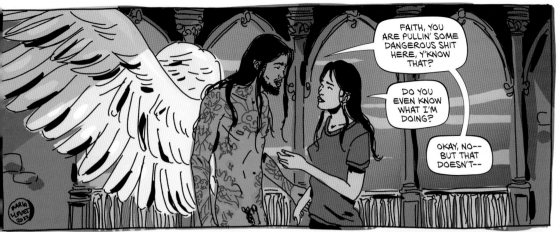

FAITH, YOU ARE PULLIN' SOME DANGEROUS SHIT HERE, Y'KNOW THAT?

DO YOU EVEN KNOW WHAT I'M DOING?

OKAY, NO-- BUT THAT DOESN'T--

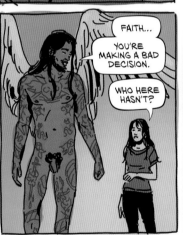

TRUST ME.

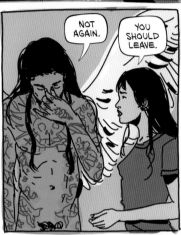

NOT AGAIN.

YOU SHOULD LEAVE.

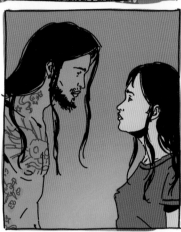

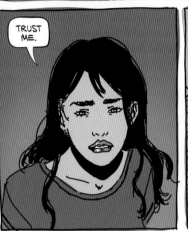

FAITH...

YOU'RE MAKING A BAD DECISION.

WHO HERE HASN'T?

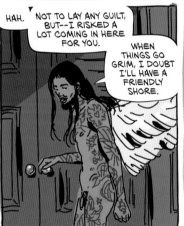

HAH.

NOT TO LAY ANY GUILT, BUT-- I RISKED A LOT COMING IN HERE FOR YOU.

WHEN THINGS GO GRIM, I DOUBT I'LL HAVE A FRIENDLY SHORE.

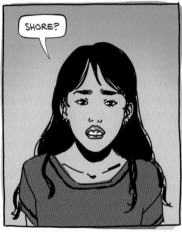

SHORE?

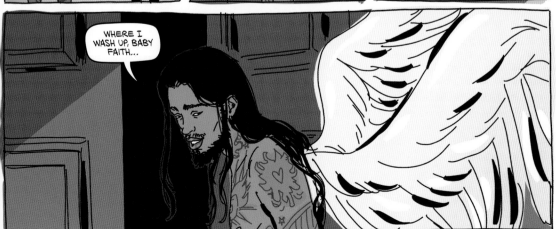

WHERE I WASH UP, BABY FAITH...

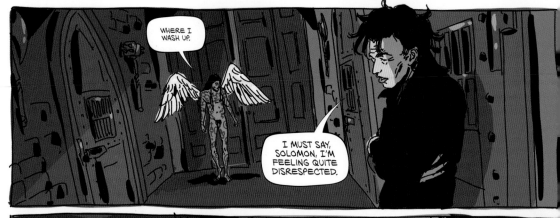

WHERE I WASH UP.

I MUST SAY, SOLOMON, I'M FEELING QUITE DISRESPECTED.

WELL, LOUIS, THAT'S ALWAYS BEEN YOUR PROBLEM.

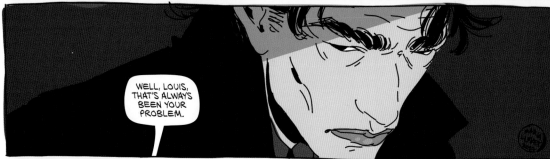

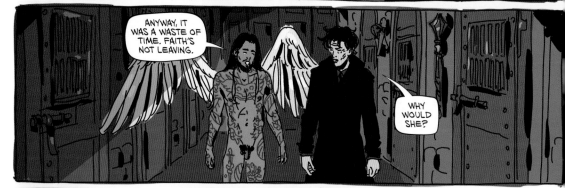

ANYWAY, IT WAS A WASTE OF TIME. FAITH'S NOT LEAVING.

WHY WOULD SHE?

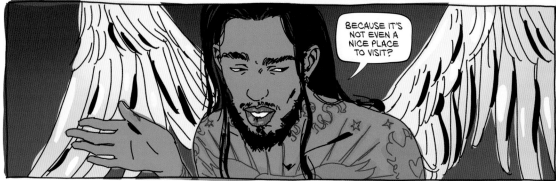

BECAUSE IT'S NOT EVEN A NICE PLACE TO VISIT?

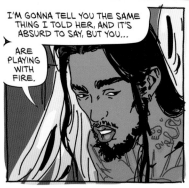

I'M GONNA TELL YOU THE SAME THING I TOLD HER, AND IT'S ABSURD TO SAY, BUT YOU...

ARE PLAYING WITH FIRE.

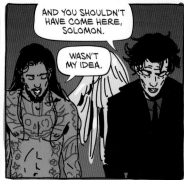

AND YOU SHOULDN'T HAVE COME HERE, SOLOMON.

WASN'T MY IDEA.

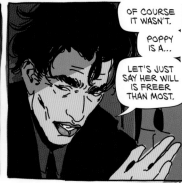

OF COURSE IT WASN'T.

POPPY IS A...

LET'S JUST SAY HER WILL IS FREER THAN MOST.

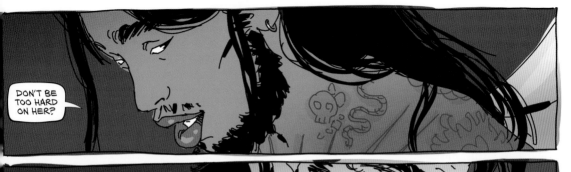

DON'T BE TOO HARD ON HER?

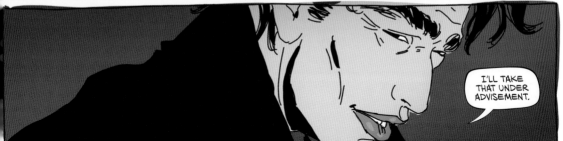

I'LL TAKE THAT UNDER ADVISEMENT.

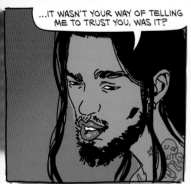

...IT WASN'T YOUR WAY OF TELLING ME TO TRUST YOU, WAS IT?

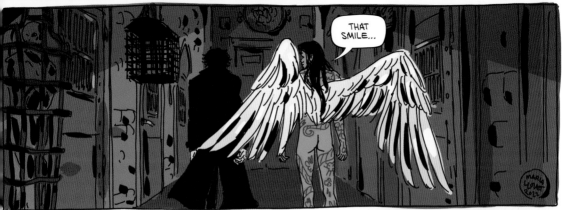

THAT SMILE...

WHY WOULD I TELL YOU THAT?

IT SEEMS LIKE EVERYONE WHO MATTERS IS.

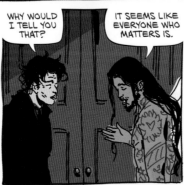

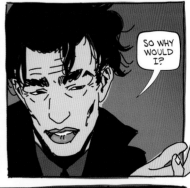

SO WHY WOULD I?

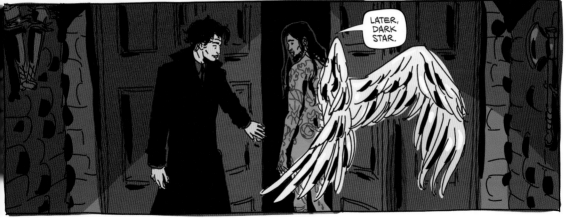

LATER, DARK STAR.

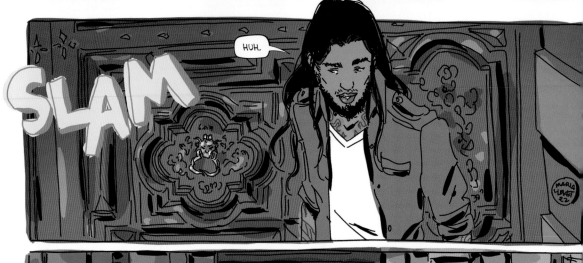

SLAM

HUH.

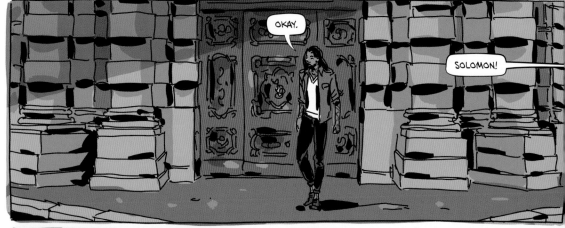

OKAY.

SOLOMON!

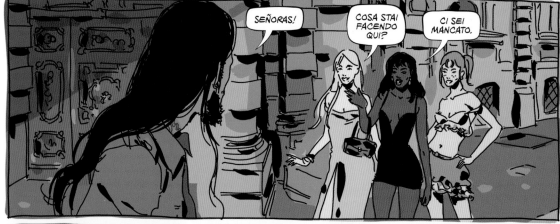

SEÑORAS!

COSA STAI FACENDO QUI?

CI SEI MANCATO.

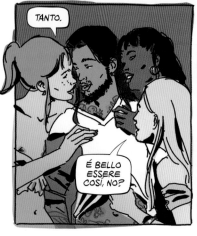

TANTO.

É BELLO ESSERE COSÍ, NO?

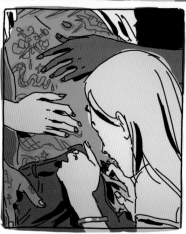

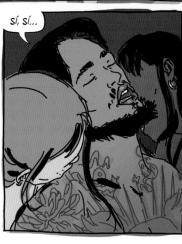

SÍ, SÍ...

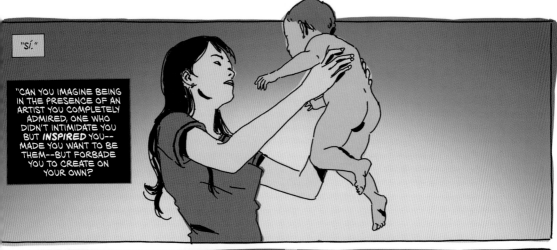

"SÍ."

"CAN YOU IMAGINE BEING IN THE PRESENCE OF AN ARTIST YOU COMPLETELY ADMIRED, ONE WHO DIDN'T INTIMIDATE YOU BUT *INSPIRED* YOU-- MADE YOU WANT TO BE THEM--BUT FORBADE YOU TO CREATE ON YOUR OWN?"

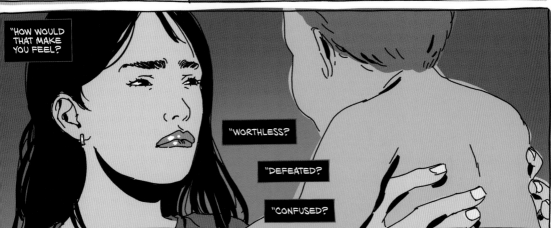

"HOW WOULD THAT MAKE YOU FEEL?"

"WORTHLESS?

"DEFEATED?

"CONFUSED?

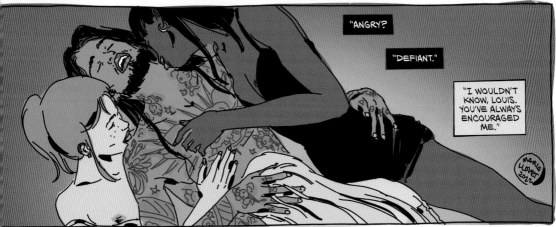

"ANGRY?

"DEFIANT."

"I WOULDN'T KNOW, LOUIS. YOU'VE ALWAYS ENCOURAGED ME."

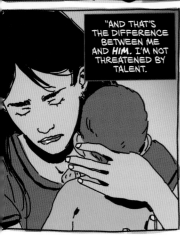

"AND THAT'S THE DIFFERENCE BETWEEN ME AND *HIM.* I'M NOT THREATENED BY TALENT.

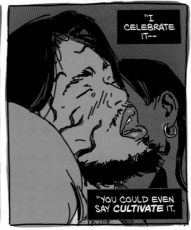

"I CELEBRATE IT--

"YOU COULD EVEN SAY *CULTIVATE* IT.

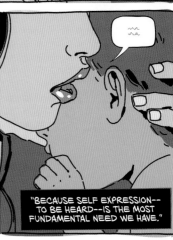

"BECAUSE SELF EXPRESSION-- TO BE HEARD--IS THE MOST FUNDAMENTAL NEED WE HAVE."

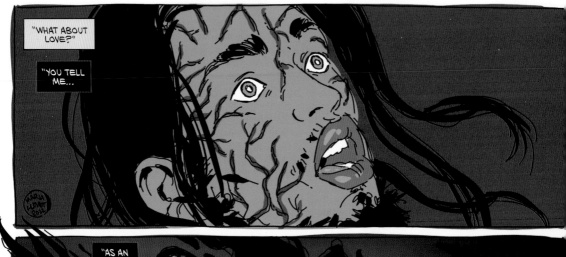

"WHAT ABOUT LOVE?"

"YOU TELL ME...

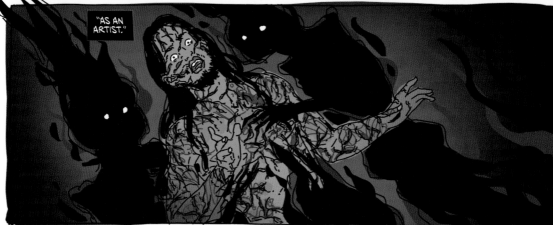

"AS AN ARTIST."

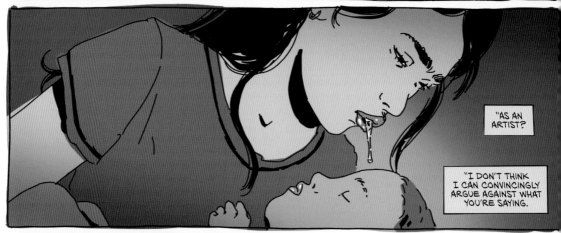

"AS AN ARTIST?

"I DON'T THINK I CAN CONVINCINGLY ARGUE AGAINST WHAT YOU'RE SAYING.

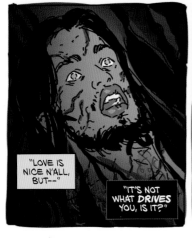

"LOVE IS NICE N'ALL, BUT--"

"IT'S NOT WHAT *DRIVES* YOU, IS IT?"

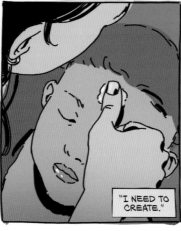

"I NEED TO CREATE."

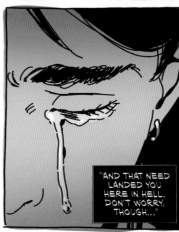

"AND THAT NEED LANDED YOU HERE IN HELL. DON'T WORRY, THOUGH..."

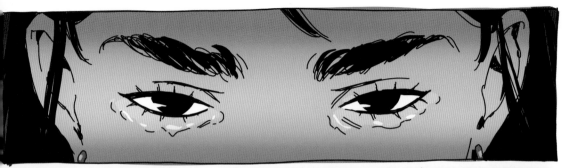

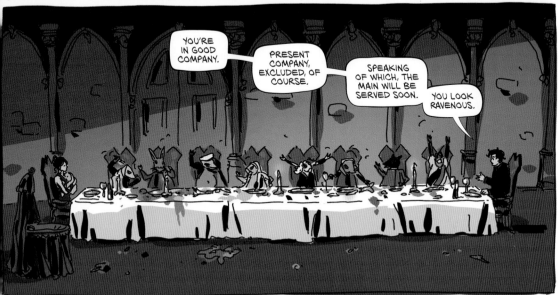

YOU'RE IN GOOD COMPANY.

PRESENT COMPANY, EXCLUDED, OF COURSE.

SPEAKING OF WHICH, THE MAIN WILL BE SERVED SOON.

YOU LOOK RAVENOUS.

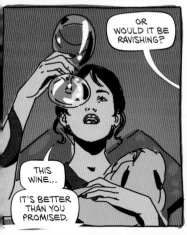

OR WOULD IT BE RAVISHING?

THIS WINE...

IT'S BETTER THAN YOU PROMISED.

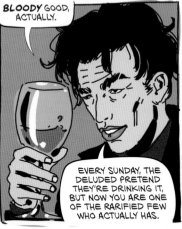

BLOODY GOOD, ACTUALLY.

EVERY SUNDAY, THE DELUDED PRETEND THEY'RE DRINKING IT, BUT NOW YOU ARE ONE OF THE RARIFIED FEW WHO ACTUALLY HAS.

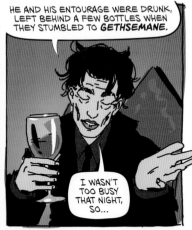

HE AND HIS ENTOURAGE WERE DRUNK, LEFT BEHIND A FEW BOTTLES WHEN THEY STUMBLED TO *GETHSEMANE*.

I WASN'T TOO BUSY THAT NIGHT, SO...

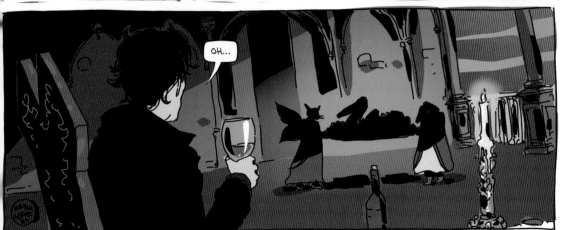

OH...

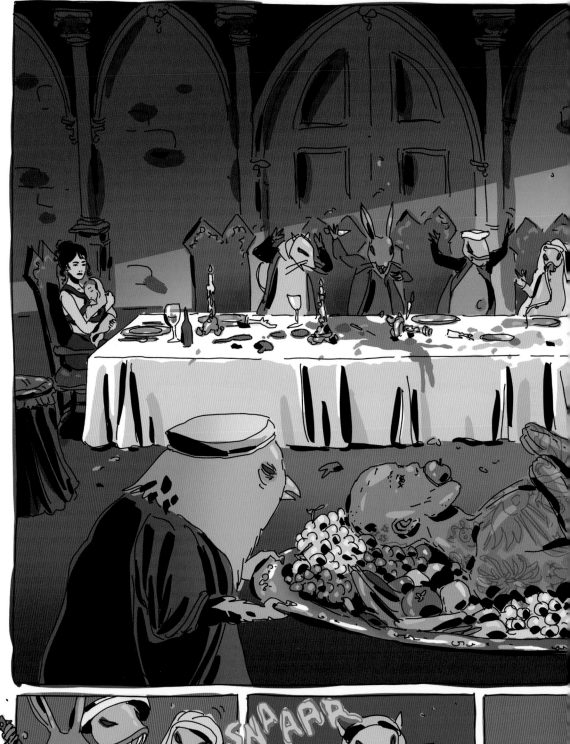

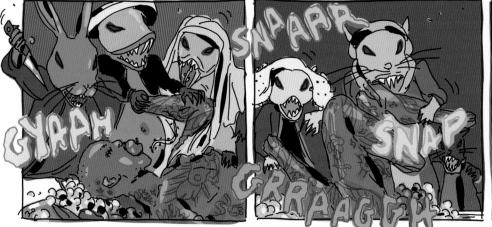

GYAAH

SNAARR

SNAP

CRRAAGGH

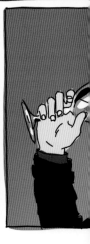

DINNER IS SERVED.
MARIA LLOVET 2022
GRBB
GYEE
WHUMP

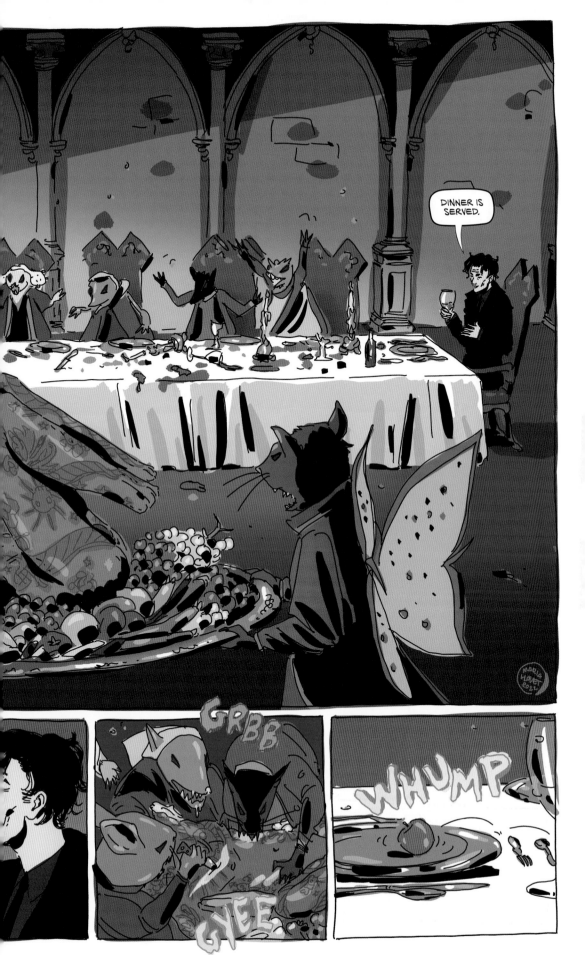

I KNOW, YOU'VE HAD HIM BEFORE, BUT NOT LIKE THIS. I THINK YOU'LL LO--
MARIA LLOVET 22
WAIT-- YOU SAID YOU'VE NEVER BEEN IN LOVE.
NO.
I SAID I'VE NEVER HAD MY HEART BROKEN.
HMM.
THAT'S SOMETHING TO DIGEST.

SOB SOB
SOB
MARIA LLOVET 2022

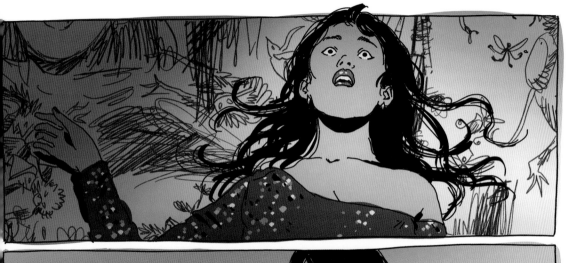

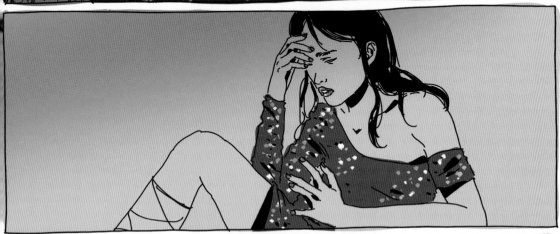

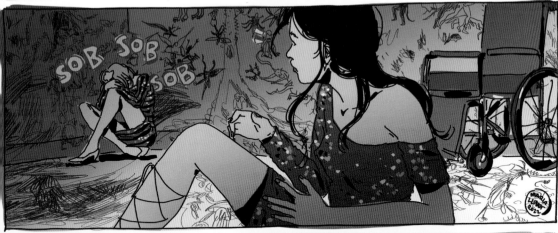

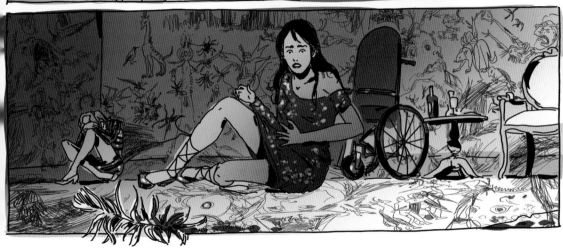

AZZARELLO
+
LLOVET
2022

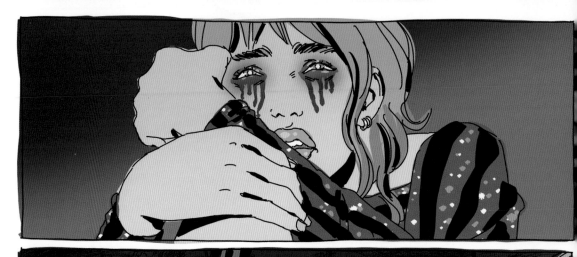

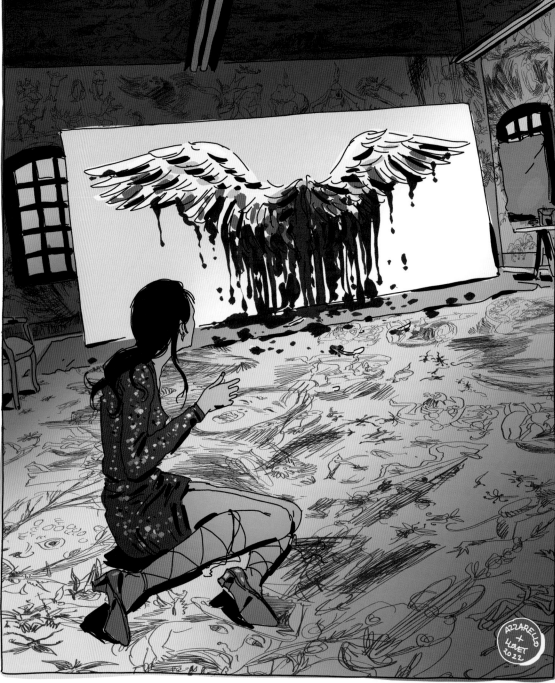

How you have **fallen** from heaven, morning star **son** of the dawn!

Isaiah 14:12

Chapter
Five

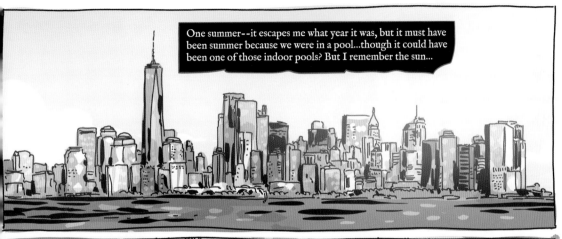

One summer--it escapes me what year it was, but it must have been summer because we were in a pool...though it could have been one of those indoor pools? But I remember the sun...

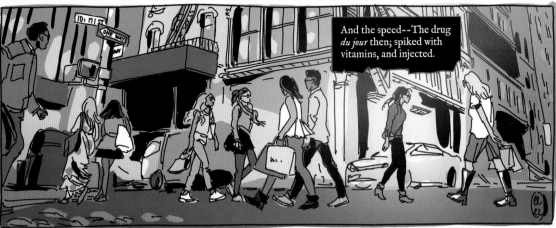

And the speed--The drug *du jour* then; spiked with vitamins, and injected.

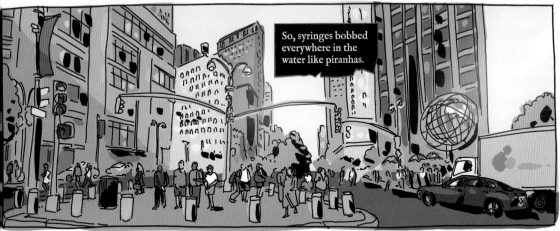

So, syringes bobbed everywhere in the water like piranhas.

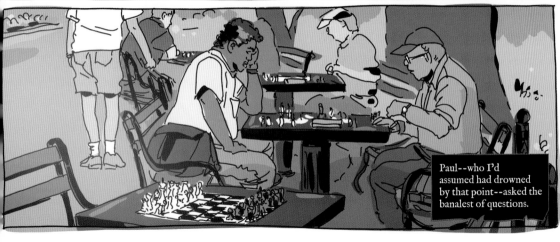

Paul--who I'd assumed had drowned by that point--asked the banalest of questions.

I looked up from my drink and I said, "You have to be kidding me--they're both the same thing, doll: obsession."

Then Liza chimed in--never an instigator, always an agitator-- and with that alluring slur of hers asked, "Okay, then, Louie, tell us: what's the opposite of obsession?"

I kept my mouth shut--well, tight around a straw, anyway, because the answer is sobering and neither *I* nor anyone else was in the mood to be *that*.

A few years later at her mother's funeral, Liza--replete with a cigarette-induced black cloud over her head--told me I still owed her an answer.

"Fear," was all I said.
Excerpt from *Louis Thorn, Dire E!* Copyright 2031. All rights reserved.
YOU'VE BEEN LOOKING FOR ME?
UM, I'VE KINDA BEEN HIDING. FROM EVERYONE.
DEARIE, IF I WANTED TO FIND **YOU,** I'D KNOW WHERE TO LOOK.
WRONG PLACE, RIGHT?

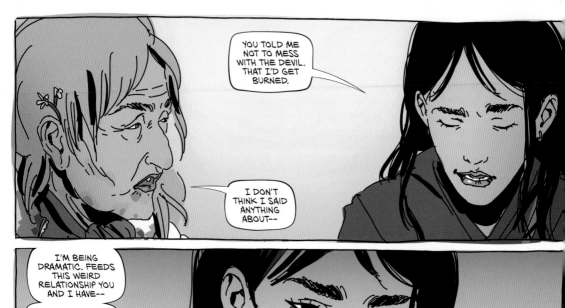

YOU TOLD ME NOT TO MESS WITH THE DEVIL. THAT I'D GET BURNED.

I DON'T THINK I SAID ANYTHING ABOUT--

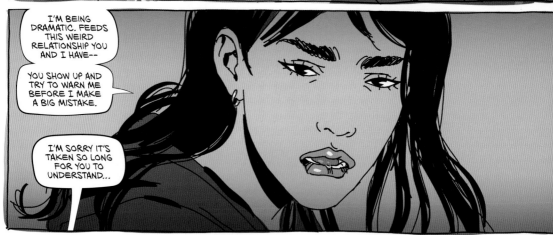

I'M BEING DRAMATIC. FEEDS THIS WEIRD RELATIONSHIP YOU AND I HAVE--

YOU SHOW UP AND TRY TO WARN ME BEFORE I MAKE A BIG MISTAKE.

I'M SORRY IT'S TAKEN SO LONG FOR YOU TO UNDERSTAND...

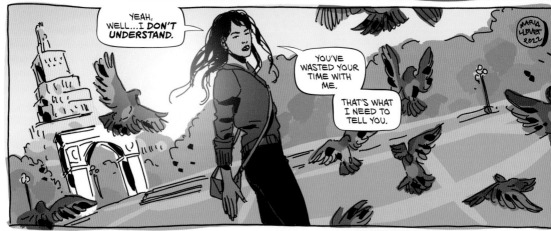

YEAH, WELL...I DON'T UNDERSTAND.

YOU'VE WASTED YOUR TIME WITH ME.

THAT'S WHAT I NEED TO TELL YOU.

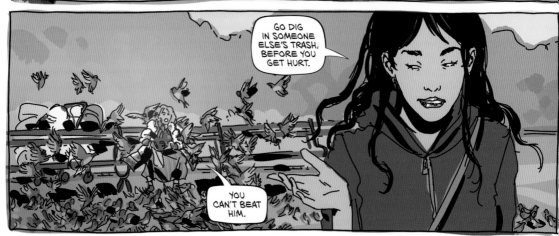

GO DIG IN SOMEONE ELSE'S TRASH, BEFORE YOU GET HURT.

YOU CAN'T BEAT HIM.

WELL, YOU KNOW WHAT THEY SAY: IF YOU CAN'T BEAT 'EM...
YOU TOLD ME YOUR NAME WAS EVE.
ONCE IT WAS.
THE APPLE... HOW DID IT TASTE?
MARIA LLOVET 2023
SILLY GIRL. IT WASN'T AN APPLE I TOOK A BITE OF.
AND WE BOTH KNOW HOW IT TASTES. FEELS.
WHAT ABOUT ITS DAUGHTER?
SHE...
I'M AFRAID FOR HER.
FOR?
NO.

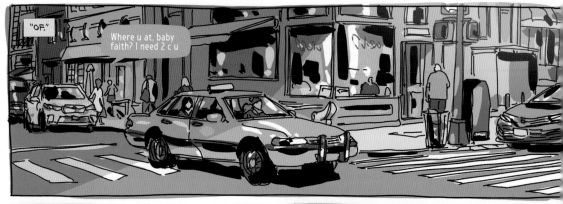

"OF."

Where u at, baby faith? I need 2 c u

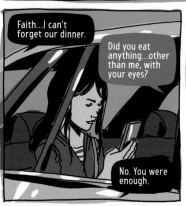

Faith...I can't forget our dinner.

Did you eat anything...other than me, with your eyes?

No. You were enough.

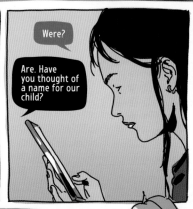

Were?

Are. Have you thought of a name for our child?

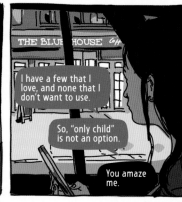

THE BLUE HOUSE

I have a few that I love, and none that I don't want to use.

So, "only child" is not an option.

You amaze me.

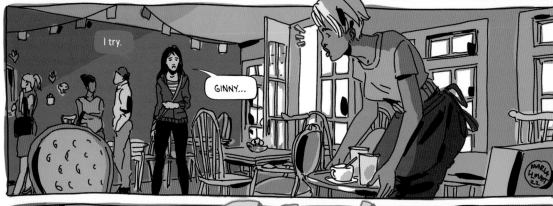

I try.

GINNY...

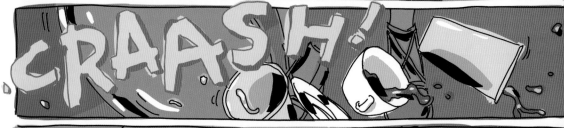

CRAASH!

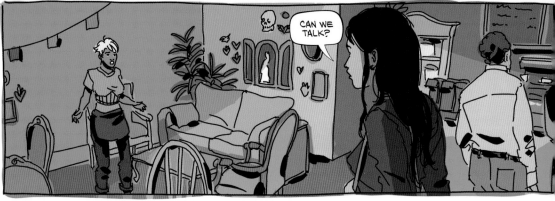

CAN WE TALK?

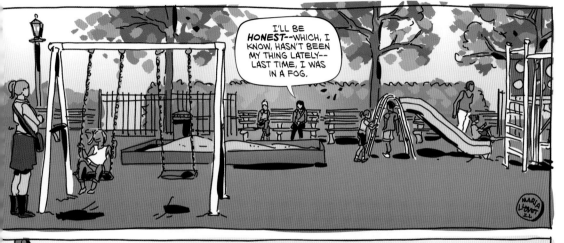

I'LL BE *HONEST*--WHICH, I KNOW, HASN'T BEEN MY THING LATELY--LAST TIME, I WAS IN A FOG.

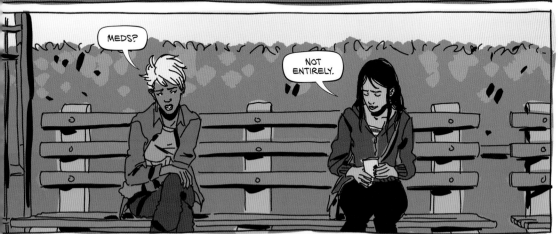

MEDS?

NOT ENTIRELY.

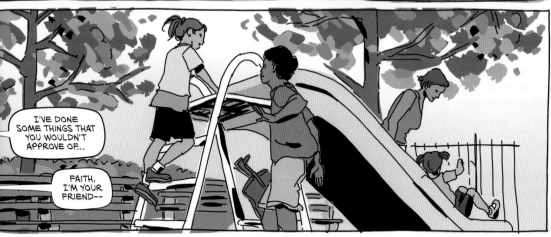

I'VE DONE SOME THINGS THAT YOU WOULDN'T APPROVE OF...

FAITH, I'M YOUR FRIEND--

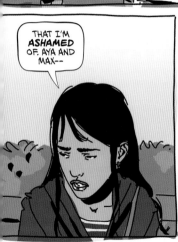

THAT I'M *ASHAMED* OF. AYA AND MAX--

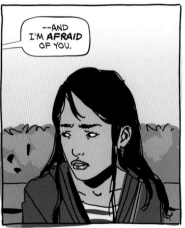

--AND I'M *AFRAID* OF YOU.

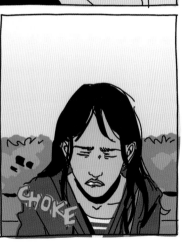

CHOKE

GINNY...I JUST WANTED TO TELL YOU THAT ONCE I SORTA GOT WHAT WAS HAPPENING...I LIKED IT. AND I WANTED TO PROTECT YOU.
THE WAY I'VE BEHAVED, IT'S NOTHING PERSONAL.
WOW. THAT HURTS.
WHA--? NO--I MEAN--
...
MARIA LLOVET 22
I'LL LEAVE.
FAITH...
I HAVE A CHILD.
IF YOU EVER HAVE ONE, YOU'LL UNDERSTAND.
I GET THAT. AND I'M SORRY.
I'M NOT.
u know I cn find u

xcept I cnt why r u magic hiding?
where r u?
MARIA LLOVET 2022
If I don't see you I'm going to kill myself.
Or everyone here. I haven't decided.
I don't want either one of those.
That hurts.
SIGH
AGAIN?
"POPPY..."

"WHAT HAVE YOU DONE?"
PRIVATE CLUB
I DIDN'T DO ANYTHING. THEY DID IT TO THEMSELVES.
WHY?
BECAUSE...
I SAID, NO MORE.
YOU'VE HAD SEX WITH ME--IS IT NOT THE **BEST EVER?** WELL, WHAT IF I SAID **NO MORE?** WHAT THEN?
?
COULD YOU LIVE WITHOUT IT? OR WOULD IT BE EASIER TO...
NEVER HAVE MET ME.

OH, PLEASE.
POPPY, THIS IS CRUEL.
THAT'S WHAT I AM, BABY FAITH.
FULFILLMENT, AND THE PIT.
A MEANS TO AN END, OR TRANSCENDENTAL SHAME, DEPENDING ON WHO'S... RELATING THE STORY.
I'M THE ORIGINAL SIN.
YOUR BABY-- MY...?
SISTER?

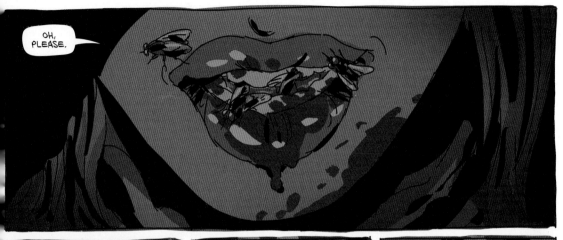

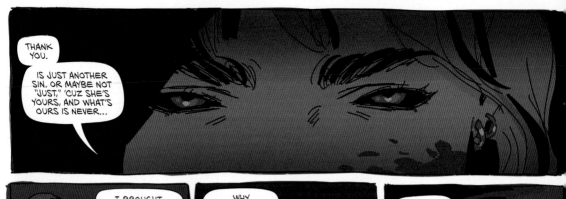

THANK YOU.

IS JUST ANOTHER SIN. OR MAYBE NOT "JUST," 'CUZ SHE'S YOURS, AND WHAT'S OURS IS NEVER...

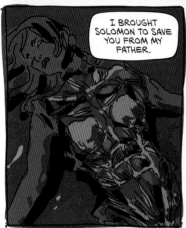

I BROUGHT SOLOMON TO SAVE YOU FROM MY FATHER.

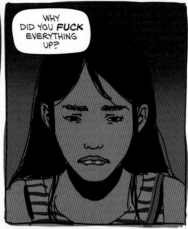

WHY DID YOU *FUCK* EVERYTHING UP?

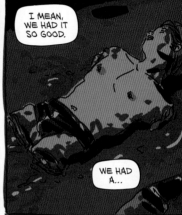

I MEAN, WE HAD IT SO GOOD.

WE HAD A...

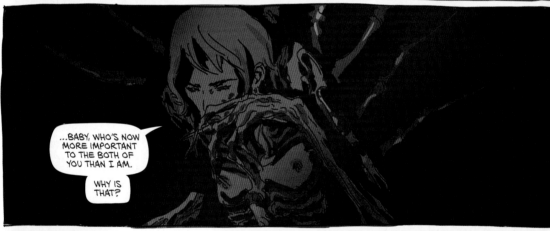

...BABY, WHO'S NOW MORE IMPORTANT TO THE BOTH OF YOU THAN I AM.

WHY IS THAT?

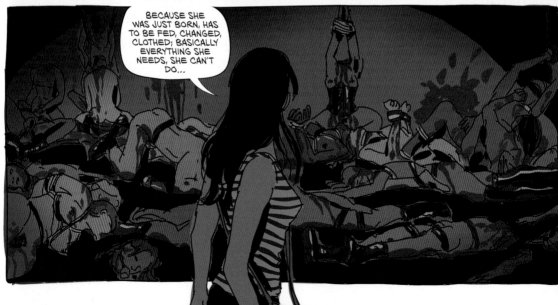

BECAUSE SHE WAS JUST BORN, HAS TO BE FED, CHANGED, CLOTHED; BASICALLY EVERYTHING SHE NEEDS, SHE CAN'T DO...

BUT SHE'S NOT HIGH-MAINTENANCE.
MARIA LLOVET 2022
GRRAAAAAGH!
HUUH!

FUUUCK.
DING!
?
WHAT IS...?
A FLASH OF BRILLIANCE...
MARIA LLOVET 2022
MINE, BY THE WAY.
THE TIME HAS COME, FAITH, TO UNVEIL THIS WORK TO THE WORLD.
OR **UNLEASH** IT. THAT MIGHT BE A BETTER WORD.

YOU KNOW, WHEN YOU FIRST STARTED SCRIBBLING ON THE WALLS, I WAS A **BIT** CONCERNED.
MARIA LLOVET 2022
I MEAN, YOU HAD A BLANK CANVAS JUST SITTING, WAITING TO BE SOLD. AND YET YOU IGNORED IT.
I WAS SEARCHING FOR THE TRUTH.
AND I CAN HAPPILY WATCH PEOPLE DO THAT ALL DAY.
DON'T TAKE THIS THE WRONG WAY, BUT AT FIRST YOU WERE ENTERTAINING, LIKE WATCHING A BUG, TRAPPED BETWEEN TWO PANES OF GLASS.
HOW IS THERE NOT A WRONG WAY TO TAKE THAT?
THEN, YOU WERE **ENTHRALLING.**
...
AND I BEGAN TO UNDERSTAND HOW WE COULD BENEFIT FROM THIS.
WE?

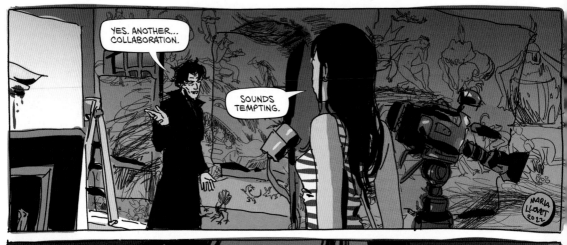

YES. ANOTHER... COLLABORATION.

SOUNDS TEMPTING.

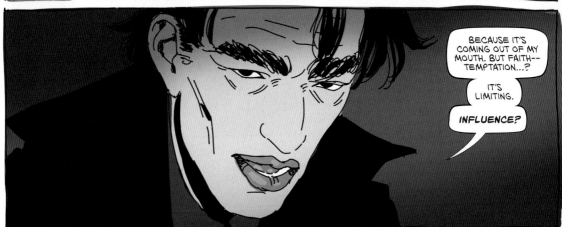

BECAUSE IT'S COMING OUT OF MY MOUTH. BUT FAITH-- TEMPTATION...?

IT'S LIMITING.

INFLUENCE?

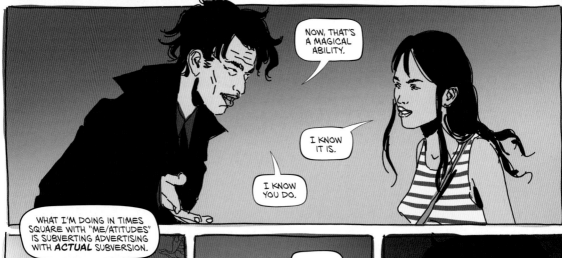

NOW, THAT'S A MAGICAL ABILITY.

I KNOW IT IS.

I KNOW YOU DO.

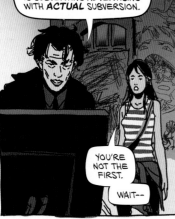

WHAT I'M DOING IN TIMES SQUARE WITH "ME/ATITUDES" IS SUBVERTING ADVERTISING WITH *ACTUAL* SUBVERSION.

YOU'RE NOT THE FIRST.

WAIT--

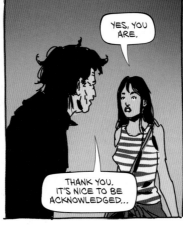

YES, YOU ARE.

THANK YOU. IT'S NICE TO BE ACKNOWLEDGED...

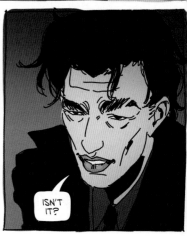

ISN'T IT?

YES, IT IS.
LOOK, LOUIS, I UNDERSTAND THAT I OWE YOU--
I MADE YOU.
OKAY...
BEFORE WE DISCUSS OUR NEXT COLLABORATION, LET'S TALK ABOUT OUR FIRST.
YOU KNEW THE TRUTH, BUT YOU KEPT IT FROM ME.
WOULD YOU HAVE BELIEVED YOUR EARS IF I TOLD YOU THE TRUTH?
YOU KEPT MY BABY FROM ME.
WELL, NOW YOU HAVE VISITATION RIGHTS. HOW'S THAT?
IT'S NOT ENOUGH.
IT HAS TO BE.
FAME, SUCCESS, THERE'S A PRICE, FAITH...

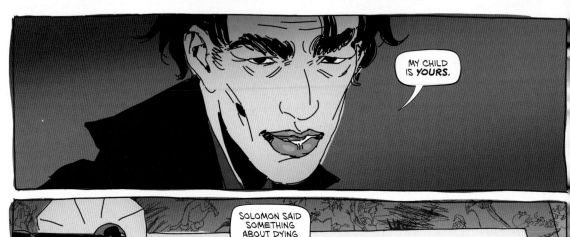

MY CHILD IS *YOURS*.

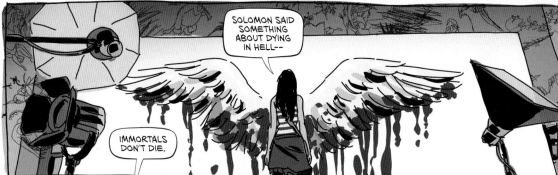

SOLOMON SAID SOMETHING ABOUT DYING IN HELL--

IMMORTALS DON'T DIE.

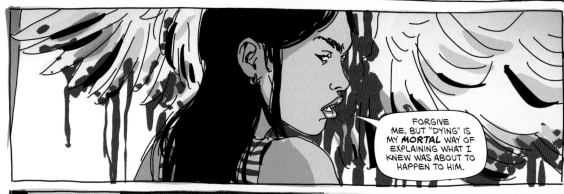

FORGIVE ME, BUT "DYING" IS MY *MORTAL* WAY OF EXPLAINING WHAT I KNEW WAS ABOUT TO HAPPEN TO HIM.

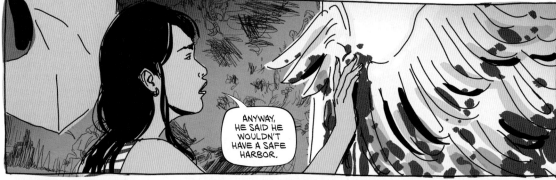

ANYWAY, HE SAID HE WOULDN'T HAVE A SAFE HARBOR.

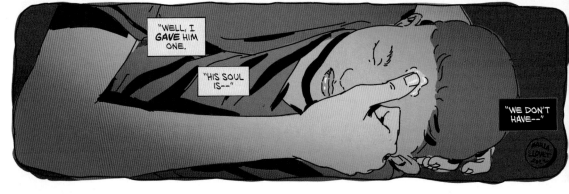

"WELL, I *GAVE* HIM ONE.

"HIS SOUL IS--"

"WE DON'T HAVE--"

SHUT UP.
OUR DAUGHTER IS DIVINE.
SHE CAN'T STAY IN HELL, CAN SHE?
GRRRR
MR. THORN, WE'RE READY FOR THE SIGNAL ON THIS END.
MARIA LLOVET 22

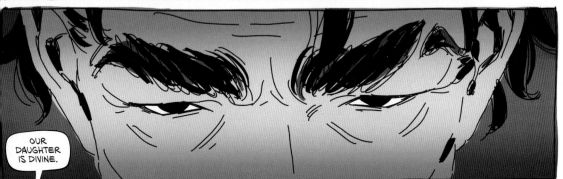

MARIA LLOVET 2022
...
SIGNAL?
THIS WORK OF YOURS, IT'S ABOUT TO BE **BROADCAST,** SEEN BY...WELL, NOT MILLIONS...
UNFORTUNATELY ART DOESN'T HAVE THAT DRAW ANYMORE.
BUT IT WILL BE **SEEN.**
IT'S NOT READY.
WHO CARES...?
CLICK
"**THEY** ARE."
PORNOGRAFREE
Broadway
The WORST thing that could HAPPEN to YOU ALREADY HAS
FREEDUMB
THESE PAINTINGS OF YOURS ARE REPULSIVE.
BUT BEAUTIFUL.
PERFECT.
REC

"ADVERTISEMENT FOR AN ETERNITY THAT NO ONE WANTS--BUT THEY'LL DESIRE. BECAUSE, FAITH, MY DEAR GIRL...
YOUR DEEPEST WISH
IS TO ATTEND YOUR OWN FUNERAL
FREEDUMB
"CONTEXT IS EVERYTHING. SO LET'S SELL HELL...
MARIA LLOVET 2022
"ALONG WITH BEAUTY, AND YOUTH, AND..."
AND...
FAITH, I'LL NEVER FORGIVE YOU.

SO SOMEONE DOES CARE.
LOUIS... YOU KNOW I'M NOTHING IF NOT ALL ABOUT INSTANT GRATIFICATION.
"SO WHY MAKE THEM WAIT FOR ETERNITY?"
AZZARELLO + LLOVET 2022

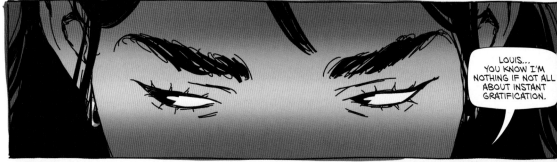

A child is a curly dimpled lunatic.

Ralph Waldo Emerson

Chapter

Six

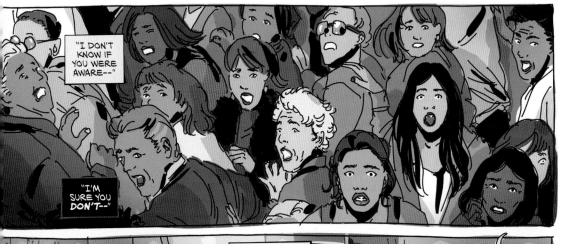

"I DON'T KNOW IF YOU WERE AWARE--"

"I'M SURE YOU *DON'T*--"

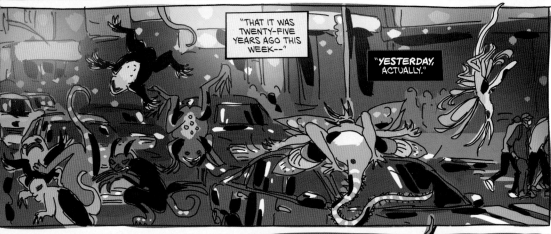

"THAT IT WAS TWENTY-FIVE YEARS AGO THIS WEEK--"

"YESTERDAY, ACTUALLY."

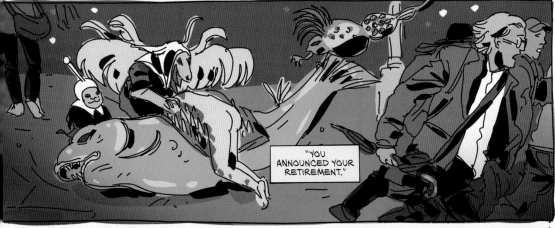

"YOU ANNOUNCED YOUR RETIREMENT."

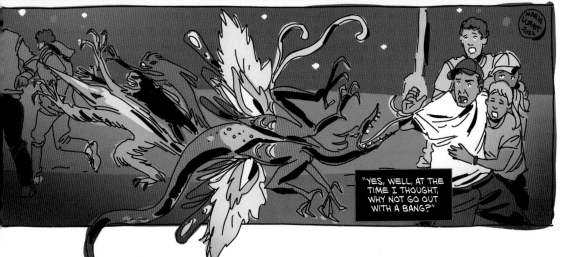

"YES, WELL, AT THE TIME I THOUGHT, WHY NOT GO OUT WITH A BANG?"

"OR A GANG BANG, TO BE MORE PRECISE."

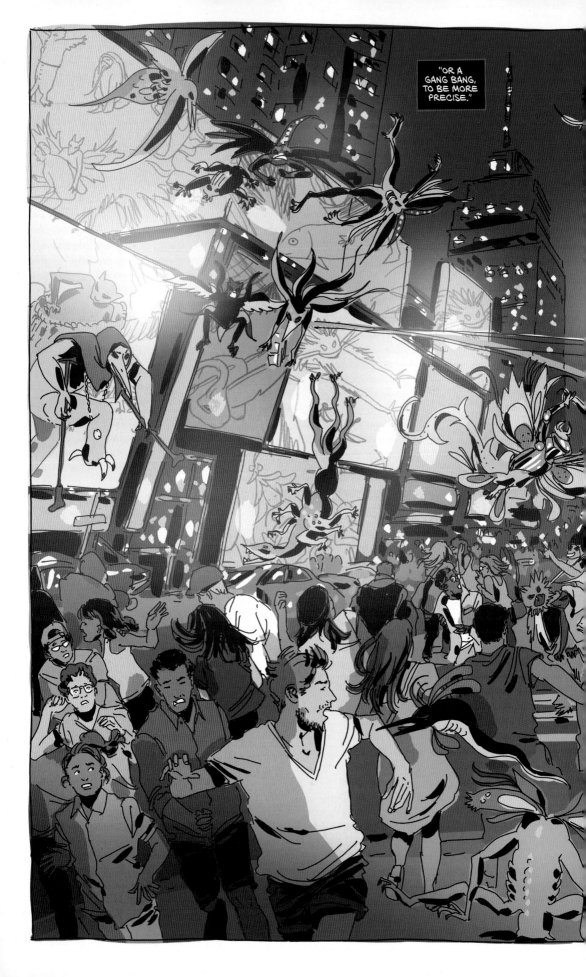

MARIA LLOVET 2022

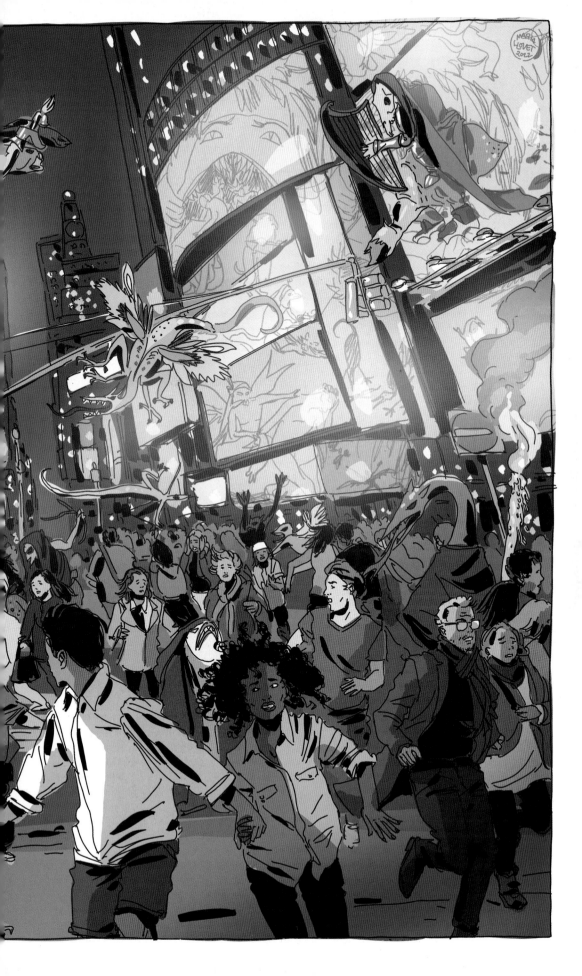

"LOUIS--"
"CALL ME MR. THORN--"
"MR. THORN, THE EXHIBIT 'ME/ATITUDES' CAUSED A RIOT."
MARIA LLOVET 2022
"I DON'T THINK YOU'RE GIVING IT ENOUGH CREDIT."
"GIVEN THE OPINION YOU **LEGENDARILY** HOLD OF YOURSELF, I'M NOT SURPRISED."
"WE'RE NOT GOING TO TALK ABOUT **HUMILITY**, ARE WE? IT'S THE ONLY LIE I FIND UTTERLY DISHONEST."

"AFTER THAT SHOW YOUR NAME WAS ON EVERYONE'S TONGUE. YET YOU STOPPED, WHY?
"WHY DOES ANYONE STOP ANYTHING? BECAUSE IT BECOMES BORING."
"TRUE, BUT HOW COULD THAT KIND OF...IT'S DIFFICULT TO CALL A 'TRAGEDY' A SUCCESS--"
"IS IT?"
MARIA LLOVET 2022
"BUT IT WAS, WASN'T IT?"
"YES, TRAGIC.
"I LOST EVERYTHING."

"...
"THAT'S NOT WHAT I WAS TALKING ABOUT, BUT YES, WITH THE RECORD NUMBER OF LAWSUITS...
MARIA LOVET 2022
"YOU WERE RUINED."
"RUINED...?"

DO I LOOK RUINED?
ACTUALLY, YOU LOOK AT PEACE.
DON'T BE INSULTING.
IS THAT WHY YOU MOVED HERE?
TO BE INSULTED?
TO FIND PEACE? TO ESCAPE?
TO HIDE?
...
TO BE ALONE.
MARIA LLOVET 2022

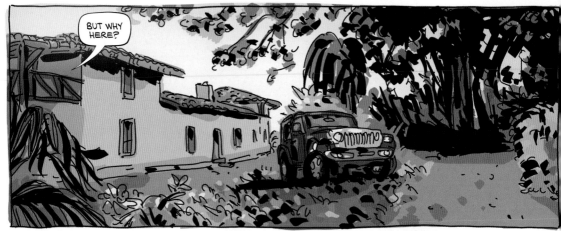

BUT WHY HERE?

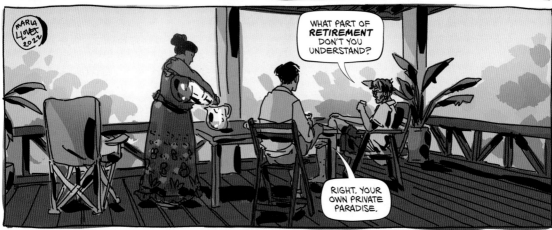

WHAT PART OF **RETIREMENT** DON'T YOU UNDERSTAND?

RIGHT. YOUR OWN PRIVATE PARADISE.

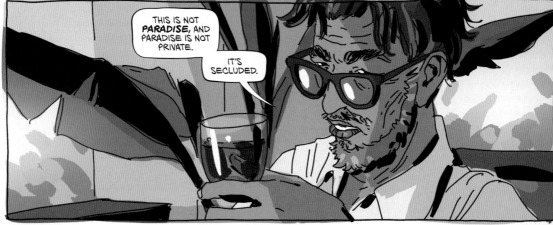

THIS IS NOT **PARADISE,** AND PARADISE IS NOT PRIVATE.

IT'S SECLUDED.

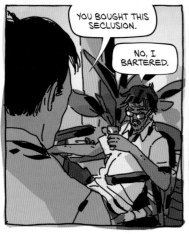

YOU BOUGHT THIS SECLUSION.

NO, I BARTERED.

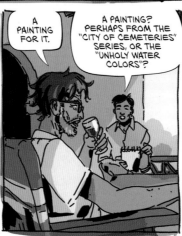

A PAINTING FOR IT.

A PAINTING? PERHAPS FROM THE "CITY OF CEMETERIES" SERIES, OR THE "UNHOLY WATER COLORS"?

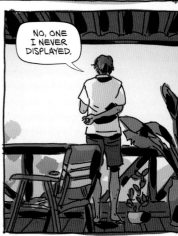

NO, ONE I NEVER DISPLAYED.

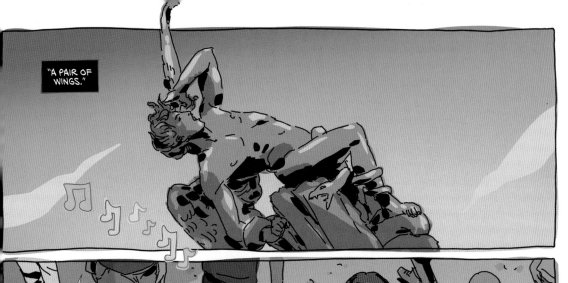

"A PAIR OF WINGS."

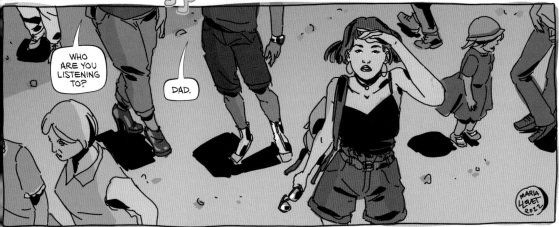

WHO ARE YOU LISTENING TO?

DAD.

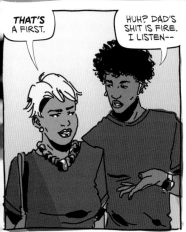

THAT'S A FIRST.

HUH? DAD'S SHIT IS FIRE. I LISTEN--

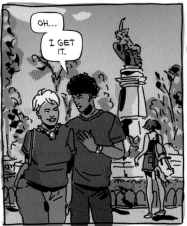

OH...

I GET IT.

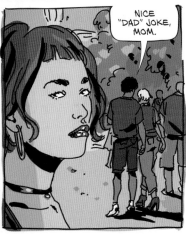

NICE "DAD" JOKE, MOM.

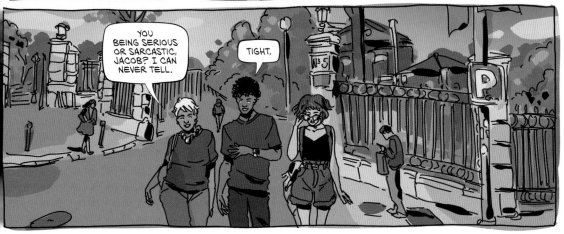

YOU BEING SERIOUS OR SARCASTIC, JACOB? I CAN NEVER TELL.

TIGHT.

...
THIS IS FUCKING BIG TIME.

15 de Abril
13 de Septiembre
FAITH: RETROSPECTIVA
FAITH: RETROSPECTIVA
15 de Abril - 13 de Septiembre
VERY, VERY BIG TIME.
WHEN DID SHE DIE?
MARIA LLOVET 2022

WHAT?!
"RETROSPECTIVE."
OH. YEAH...
"I HAD A THOUGHT..."

EVERYONE IN THE WORLD HAS SEEN THIS PAINTING FROM THE FRONT. I WANT THEM TO SEE IT FROM THE BACK. CAN WE TURN--
FAITH!
GINNY! SO GOOD TO SEE YOU.
'SUP, AUNTIE FAITH?
SUGAR, JACOB!
AND OH MY, SALLY MAE--WHAT HAVE YOU DONE TO YOUR HAIR? I LOVE IT!
THANK YOU...
MOM.
"WHAT HAPPENED IN TIMES SQUARE?"
MARIA LLOVET 2022

WHY CAN'T YOU JUST ACCEPT THAT IT DID HAPPEN?
BECAUSE I WANT TO KNOW.
WHY?
BECAUSE THE REALITY WAS SO DIFFERENT FROM...
MARIA LLOVET 2022
REALITY?
YOU COULD PUT IT THAT WAY...
"... OR I COULD CALL IT WHAT IT WAS CALLED AT THE TIME: MASS HYSTERIA.
"MASS HYPNOSIS.
"THE GRANDEST ILLUSION OF ALL TIME."

QUARTER OF A CENTURY LATER, NO ONE HAS BEEN ABLE TO EXPLAIN HOW PEOPLE SAW WHAT YOU MADE THEM SEE.
PEOPLE ARE BLIND.
MARIA LLOVET 2021
TO REALITY.
BUT IT WASN'T REAL. MULTIPLE CAMERAS CAPTURED PEOPLE--
REACTING-- FOR **REAL.**
SO YOU GOT THE RESPONSE YOU WERE AFTER? THAT SEEMS INCREDIBLY SELF-DESTRUCTIVE.
POINT BEING?
THAT IF NOT FOR ALL THE INJURIES AND THE LAWSUITS, IN ***MY*** OPINION, "ME/ATITUDES" RANKS--
YOUR OPINION IS GOAT SHIT.
I WAS ABOUT TO COMPLIMENT YOUR WORK.
AND? THAT DOESN'T CHANGE ***MY*** OPINION IN THE LEAST...

"BUT DO GO ON."
DO YOU KNOW HOW LONG I'VE BEEN PISSED AT YOU?
OOF...
ALL THE TEENAGE YEARS?
THEM. AND THEN SOME.
SALLY MAE--
THAT **NAME,** TOO--WHAT WERE YOU THINKING?
NOT ONLY OF YOU.
YOU ABANDONED ME.
I **SAVED** YOU FIRST.
MARIA LLOVET 2022
...I'M BEGINNING TO GET THAT.
IT'S LIKE...I WAS BORN TWENTY-FIVE YEARS AGO, BUT I'VE EXISTED NEARLY FOREVER.

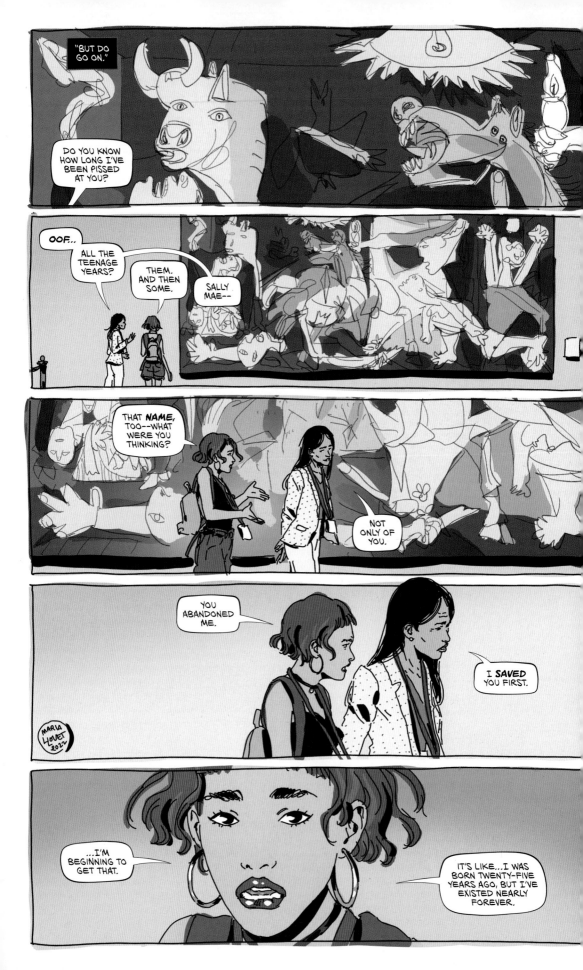

I THINK...I HAVE--IT'S NOT QUITE A DREAM--BUT I REMEMBER EXPLAINING MY EXISTENCE TO YOU.
YOU DID.
WHAT WAS YOUR BIG TAKEAWAY?
THAT YOU DIDN'T HAVE FREE WILL.
...
I DO NOW. THANKS.
MY PLEASURE.
SO THEN, WHY DID YOU ABANDON ME?
I DIDN'T HAVE A CHOICE.
AND I WISH YOU WOULD STOP BEING DRAMATIC. YOU WERE RAISED IN PARIS BY THE MOST CAPABLE WOMAN I'VE EVER KNOWN.
I'M NOT COMPLAINING. I LOVE GINNY, AND I KNOW SHE LOVES ME. WHAT I DON'T KNOW--
IS IF I LOVE YOU? SO MUCH. I DID, I DO...
BUT I HAD A CHOICE TO MAKE.
MARIA LLOVET 2022
"YOU QUIT MAKING ART..."

DID I?
THEN TEN YEARS LATER AN AUTOBIOGRAPHY--WHICH AT THE TIME WAS RUMORED TO BE PUBLISHED POSTHUMOUSLY...
THEY WISH.
AND NOW THIS INTERVIEW--WHICH I DON'T BELIEVE HAS ANYTHING TO DO WITH THEIR WISHES, AND EVERYTHING TO DO WITH YOURS.
WHAT DO YOU WISH TO SHOW US?
YOUR SHOES ARE SPLATTERED WITH PAINT.
MARIA LLOVET 2022
HOW OBSERVANT.
BEEP

"WHAT'S THIS?"
"OH, I DIDN'T REALIZE HOW LATE IT'S GOTTEN. I'M THROWING A LITTLE PARTY HERE TONIGHT."
I'M SORRY, THANK YOU FOR--
TELL ME, WHEN YOU DISCOVERED I WAS HERE, YOU BEGGED, PLEADED--
IF I REMEMBER RIGHT, YOUR REPRESENTATIVE ASKED IF YOU WOULD SELL YOUR SOUL FOR THIS INTERVIEW.
AND YOU AGREED.
METAPHORICALLY.
WHY DON'T YOU STICK AROUND...?
MARIA LLOVET 2022

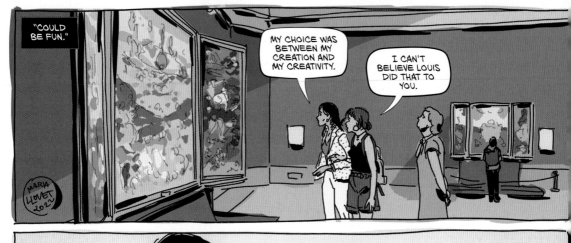

"COULD BE FUN."

MY CHOICE WAS BETWEEN MY CREATION AND MY CREATIVITY.

I CAN'T BELIEVE LOUIS DID THAT TO YOU.

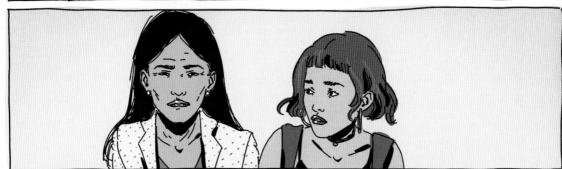

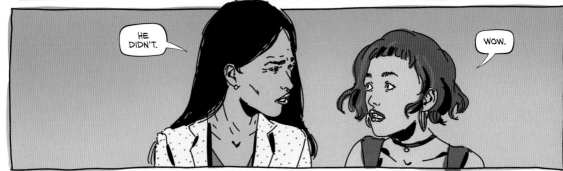

HE DIDN'T.

WOW.

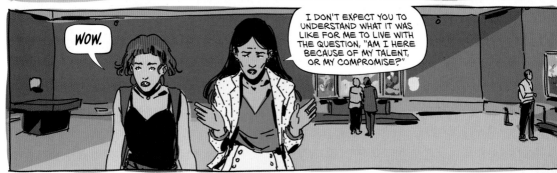

WOW.

I DON'T EXPECT YOU TO UNDERSTAND WHAT IT WAS LIKE FOR ME TO LIVE WITH THE QUESTION, "AM I HERE BECAUSE OF MY TALENT, OR MY COMPROMISE?"

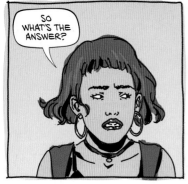

SO WHAT'S THE ANSWER?

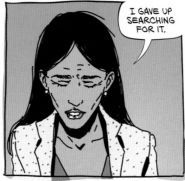

I GAVE UP SEARCHING FOR IT.

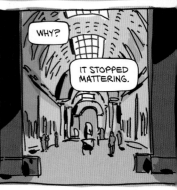

WHY?

IT STOPPED MATTERING.

THAT MUST BE HARD TO ADMIT.
NOT REALLY.
DO YOU REGRET YOUR CHOICE?
BZZZ
I'M SORRY.
HAVE YOU SEEN HIM?
MARIA LLOVET 2022
HEAVENS, NO.
BUT YOU WILL.
BZZZZ
I KNOW. LIKE MOST...
...WHEN I DIE.

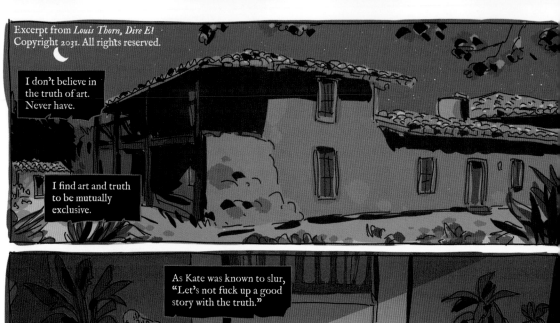

I don't believe in
the truth of art.
Never have.

I find art and truth
to be mutually
exclusive.

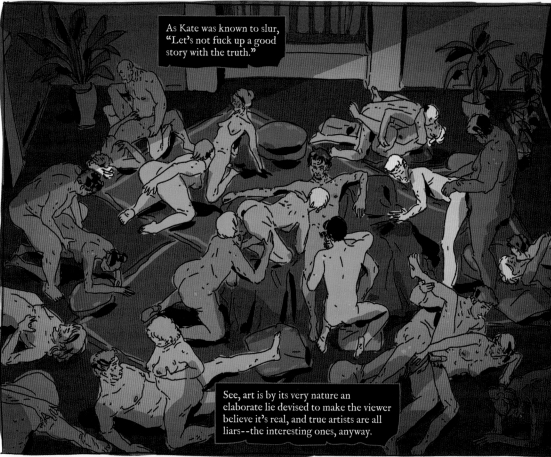

As Kate was known to slur,
"Let's not fuck up a good
story with the truth."

See, art is by its very nature an
elaborate lie devised to make the viewer
believe it's real, and true artists are all
liars--the interesting ones, anyway.

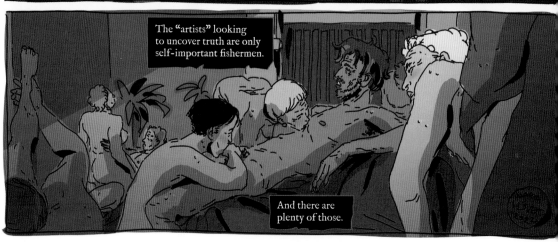

The "artists" looking
to uncover truth are only
self-important fishermen.

And there are
plenty of those.

You want truth? Look around yourself. Touch that person.
Look at the sky.
MARIA LLOVET 22
Look beyond the sky.
Beyond the horizon.
Look at the mountains, and the oceans, and all the sand on all the beaches.
Don't look within...
...because it's not there.

The *Creator* is the only artist whose medium is the truth.
And their masterpiece?
Why, the devil, of course.
The devil is God's masterpiece.
AZZARELLO + LLOVET 2022

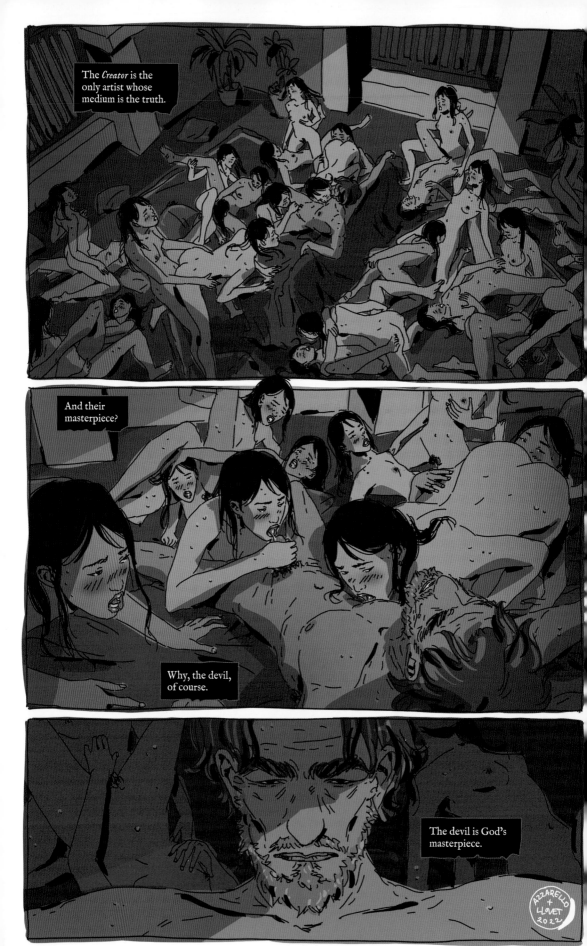

Faithless
is he that says
farewell
when the road
darkens.

J.R.R. Tolkien

MARIA
LLOVET
2021

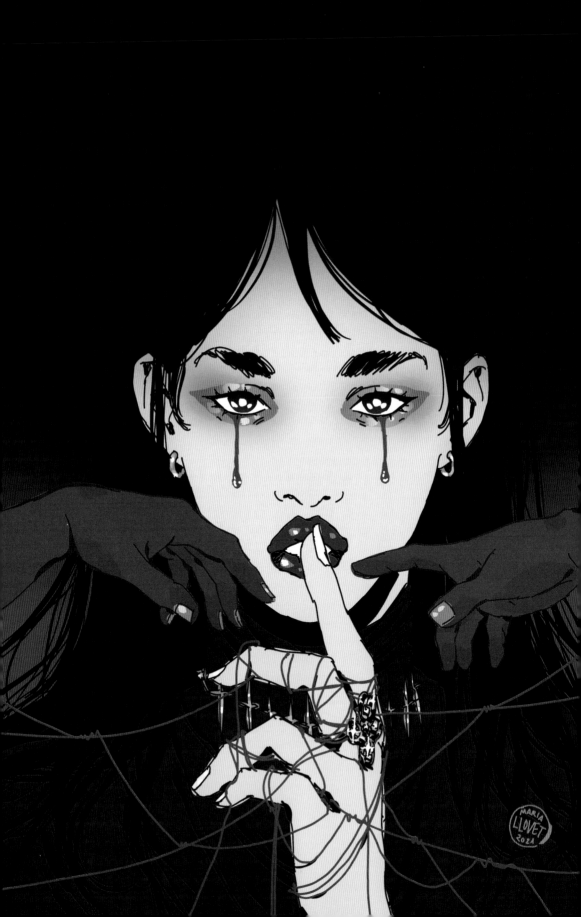

MARIA
LLOVET
2021

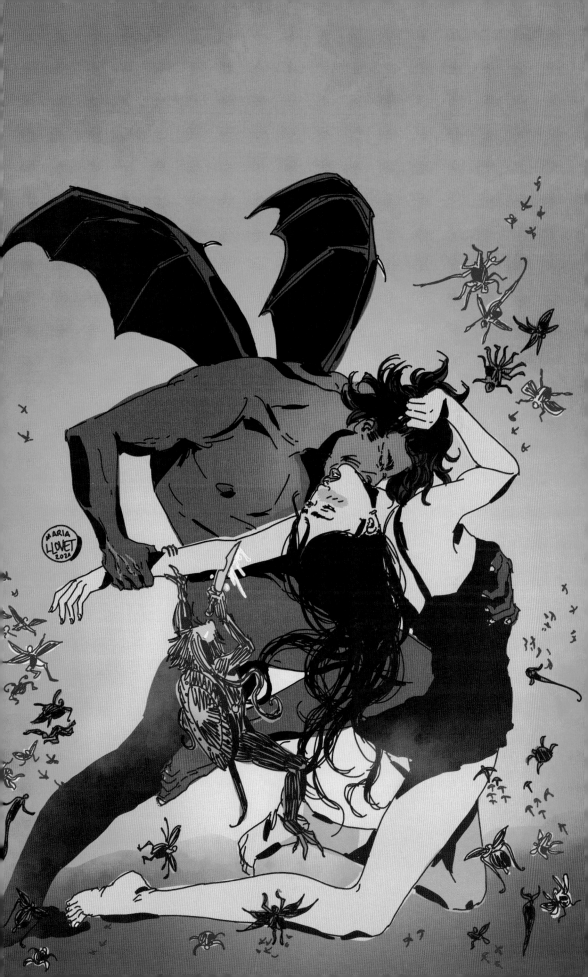

MARIA
LLOVET
2021

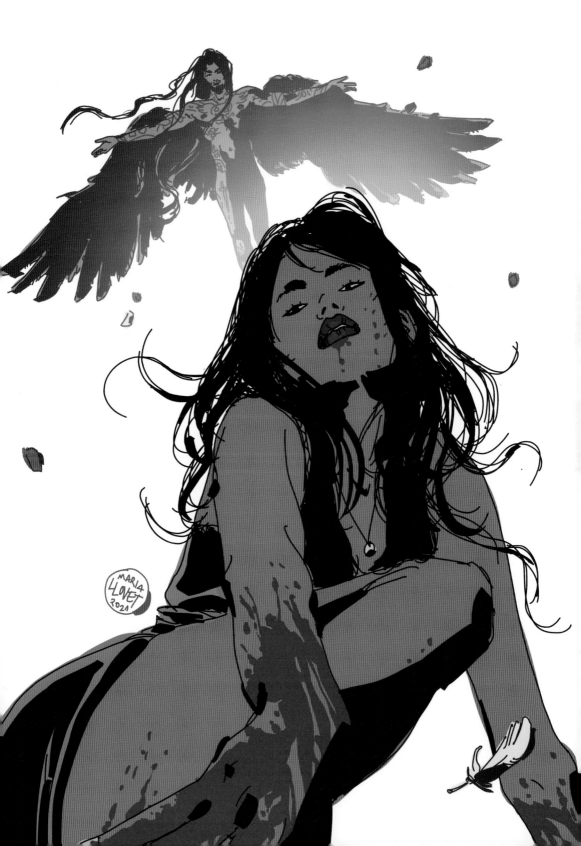

With following art credited in order of appearance:
Jenny Frison, Paulina Ganucheau, Tula Lotay,
Stephanie Hans, Abigail Jill Harding, and Cathy Kwan

MARIA
LLOVET
2021

BOOM! Studios
Brian Azzarello · Maria Llovet
No
FAITHLESS III™
"The path to paradise begins in hell." —Dante Alighieri
666
SPRING
FASHION
TIPS
IDLE HANDS ARE THE
DEVIL'S PLAYTHINGS
AND THAT'S WHAT WE LIKE ABOUT THEM!

EXIT

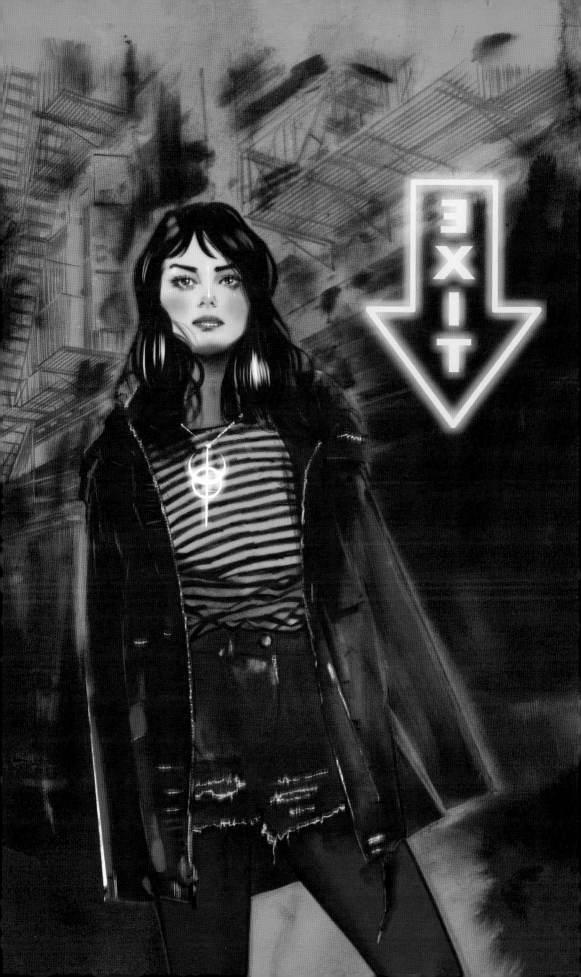

Faithless
SH

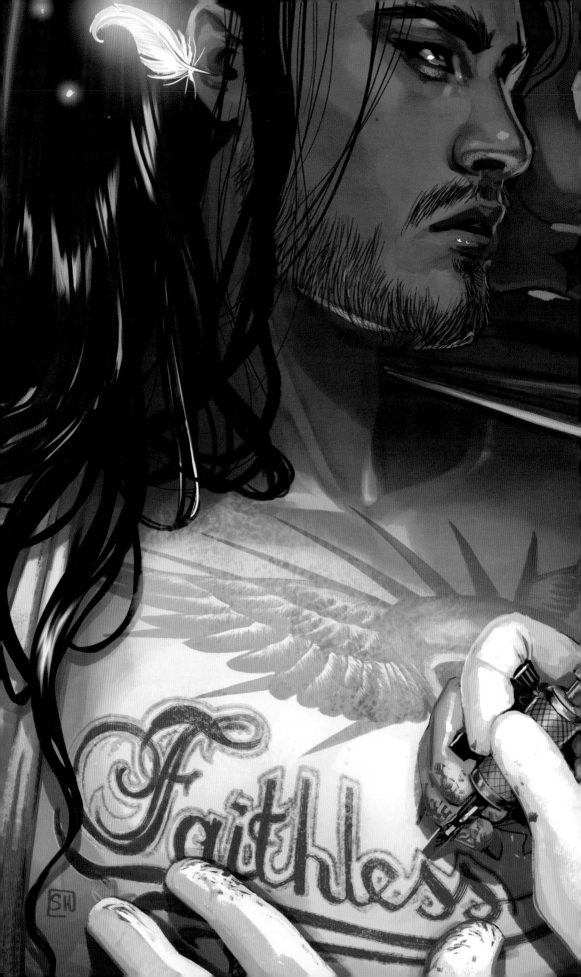